The Children's Encyclopedia

of BIBLE
PEOPLE

Written by Mark Water
Illustrations by Karen Donnelly

ZondervanPublishingHouse
Grand Rapids, Michigan

A Division of HarperCollins*Publishers*

The Children's Encyclopedia
of Bible People

Copyright © 1995 Hunt & Thorpe
Text © Mark Water
Illustrations © Karen Donnelly

Originally published by Hunt & Thorpe 1995

Designed by
The Bridgewater Book Company
Designer *Sarah Bentley*
Managing Editor *Anna Clarkson*
Editor *Fiona Corbridge*
Page make-up *Chris Lanaway*
Text consultant *Derek Williams*

ISBN 0-310-21106-9

In the United States this book is published by:
Zondervan Publishing House
Grand Rapids, Michigan 49530

Printed and bound in the USA

Acknowledgements
Bible quotations are from:
The Holy Bible, New International Version,
© 1973, 1978, 1984 by International Bible
Society. Used by permission of Hodder and
Stoughton. International Children's Bible, New
Century Version (Anglicized Edition),
© 1991 Word (UK) Ltd. Used by permission.

CONTENTS

ABOUT THIS BOOK

This book is in chronological order – it follows the sequence of events, but you don't have to start at the beginning: you can start anywhere, depending on what you want to read about. The title at the top of each page gives you the main subject for that page. You can find which page you need by looking in the contents page, or in the index at the end of this book.

The Bible was written by many different people over a long period of time. In this book you can read about some of the people, places and events which appear in the Bible. You can start reading right at the beginning with Adam, through to King David, Jesus and Paul.

Enjoy the colourful, clearly drawn artwork – it shows you what people wore in Bible times, how they lived and travelled, and also what we think the different characters might have looked like.

Bible Search

- Noah and the Flood: **Genesis 6–8**

- The rainbow: **Genesis 9:8–17**

- Noah's faith: **Hebrews 11:7**

When you read these pages you may think, 'Does the Bible really say that?' The best thing you can do is to find out for yourself! Most of the pages have a Bible Search so that you can look up the verses in your own Bible.

ANY QUESTIONS

These questions help you examine the text more closely, and to think about some of the Bible's teachings.

On many pages you will see the words 'See also' or 'To find out more'. By turning to the suggested pages, you can follow a story or a subject through the book. For example, read about Abraham, then turn to Lot, Isaac and Sarah, then to Genesis, and so on.

THE BIBLE
There are 66 books in the Bible. This may seem like a lot of pages, but there is an easy system for finding your way around:

- Each Bible book is split up into chapters, and each chapter has a number. Exodus 1 means the first chapter of the Book of Exodus. Usually these numbers are set at the top of each page in your Bible.
- Each chapter is split up into short sections of one or two lines. These are called verses. Verses also have numbers. The verse numbers are the small numbers on each page. So Exodus 1:12 means verse 12 of chapter 1 of the Book of Exodus.

BC refers to all the years before Jesus was born: 500 BC means 500 years before Jesus was born. AD refers to all the years after Jesus was born.
All the dates of events in the Old Testament are 'BC'; all the dates in the New Testament are 'AD'.

BIBLE FACTS

The Bible isn't like any other book in the world. This is because its writers were inspired by God. All the different writings give us a true picture of God, and of how he wants us to live. Without the Bible, we would know almost nothing about Jesus and his teaching.

The Bible isn't like any other book in the world

FACT FILE

- The Bible contains sixty-six books.
- It was written over a period of 1,500 years.
- Over thirty-five people wrote the books.
- The Old Testament was first written in Hebrew; the New Testament was first written in Greek.
- The Bible has sold more copies than any other book in the world.

The Bible was written by many different people

YEAST

One day, Jesus spoke about yeast. He said, 'A woman took some yeast and mixed it with a lot of flour to make bread. All the flour rose.'

God's word in the Bible is like that yeast. If we read it, think about it, and act on it, it changes our lives.

God's word is like yeast!

FINDING HELP

The Bible is not always easy to understand. But God has promised that the Holy Spirit will help us to understand it. A good place to begin is with the teaching and life of Jesus in the Gospels.

- Friends of Jesus: **John 15:14**
- Pray for enemies: **Matthew 5:44**
- Yeast: **Matthew 13:33**
- The Spirit as guide: **John 16:12–16**

HOW CAN THE BIBLE HELP ME?

Here's an example of how you can find help in the Bible. Suppose your best friend makes fun of you. You feel upset and lonely, and pray to Jesus. Then you remember:

- One of Jesus' best friends gave him away to his enemies. He knows how you feel.
- Jesus said, 'You are my friends if you do what I say.' You are not alone. Jesus is with you.
- Jesus said, 'Pray for those who treat you badly.' Pray for your friend, and decide not to gossip about it.

When your best friend makes fun of you

5

OLD TESTAMENT STORY

T he Old Testament is God's story. In its pages we see God at work in the lives of ordinary and extraordinary people. God did not only give a list of rules to obey. He showed what happened when people lived as he wanted, and what happened when they ignored him.

Most of all, we see how God prepared his people for the coming of Jesus. This chart shows some of the important events in the history of God's people, and the order in which they came.

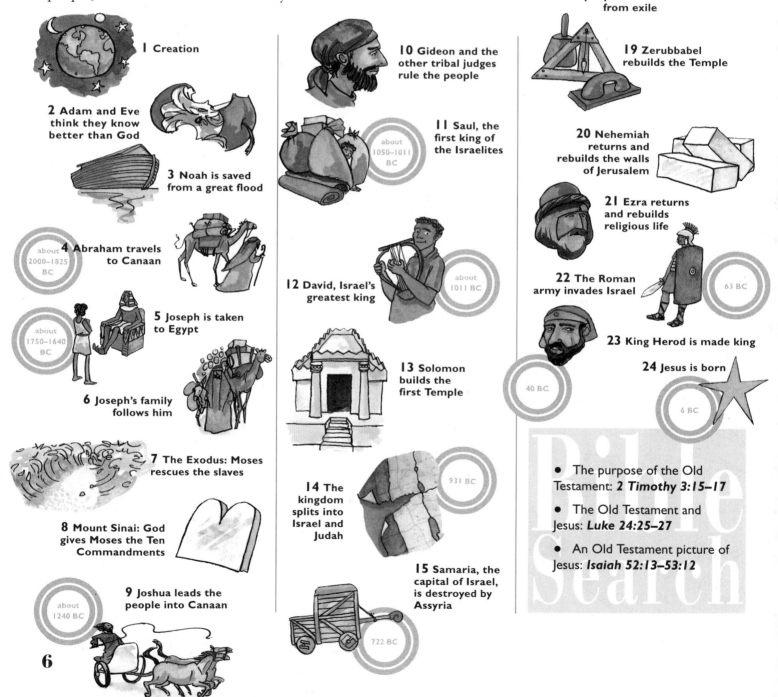

587 BC

16 Jerusalem, the capital of Judah, is destroyed by Babylon

17 Exile: the Israelite people are taken away as prisoners and spend 70 years in Babylonia

538 BC

18 The first people return from exile

1 Creation

2 Adam and Eve think they know better than God

3 Noah is saved from a great flood

about 2000–1825 BC

4 Abraham travels to Canaan

about 1750–1640 BC

5 Joseph is taken to Egypt

6 Joseph's family follows him

7 The Exodus: Moses rescues the slaves

8 Mount Sinai: God gives Moses the Ten Commandments

about 1240 BC

9 Joshua leads the people into Canaan

10 Gideon and the other tribal judges rule the people

about 1050–1011 BC

11 Saul, the first king of the Israelites

12 David, Israel's greatest king

about 1011 BC

13 Solomon builds the first Temple

931 BC

14 The kingdom splits into Israel and Judah

722 BC

15 Samaria, the capital of Israel, is destroyed by Assyria

19 Zerubbabel rebuilds the Temple

20 Nehemiah returns and rebuilds the walls of Jerusalem

21 Ezra returns and rebuilds religious life

22 The Roman army invades Israel

63 BC

23 King Herod is made king

40 BC

24 Jesus is born

6 BC

- The purpose of the Old Testament: *2 Timothy 3:15–17*

- The Old Testament and Jesus: *Luke 24:25–27*

- An Old Testament picture of Jesus: *Isaiah 52:13–53:12*

Bible Search

6

CREATION

E verything we make is made out of something else. But God made planet Earth, space, the stars and time out of nothing – just by speaking.

He made the Earth as a home for men and women and he put them in charge. At every stage God said that everything was good. It was all exactly as he wanted it. It was like watching plants grow.

God created every plant and creature

Looking at the planets

IN THE BEGINNING

How we think the world began affects everything else we think and do. In the Bible it explains this. It says God is very powerful. He knows what is best for us and we must obey and trust him. Earth is the home God gave us, and we must look after our planet.

The Bible also tells us that we need to respect one another as we are all made and loved by God. God sent Jesus to save the world he loves. We should be hopeful about the future.

WHAT HAPPENED WHEN

In the beginning of the story of the creation, there was a shapeless mass of energy called chaos. Then God created the world day by day:

Day One. God created light, and made day and night.

Day Two. God created the sky and air.

Day Three. God created land, sea, grass, plants and trees.

Day Four. God created the sun, moon and stars, and the seasons.

Day Five. God created birds and fish.

Day Six. God created animals, insects, reptiles and people.

Day Seven. God rested.

In one of the psalms it says that when we look at God's world, we want to worship him because it is so beautiful. 'Look at the sea, so big and wide, its creatures large and small cannot be counted.' (Psalm 95:5–6)

ANY QUESTIONS
1 What do scientists say about creation? To find out more, look at the opposite page.
2 What difference does this make?

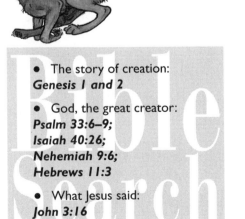

Bible **S**earch

● The story of creation: *Genesis 1 and 2*

● God, the great creator: *Psalm 33:6–9; Isaiah 40:26; Nehemiah 9:6; Hebrews 11:3*

● What Jesus said: *John 3:16*

ADAM AND EVE
FIRST MAN AND WOMAN

When God had made the Earth and its living creatures, he made a man. The man was called Adam. God didn't want Adam to be lonely, so he decided to make a partner for him. While Adam was asleep, God took one of his ribs and made it into a woman called Eve. Adam and Eve were both equally important to God. Neither Adam nor Eve wore clothes.

Adam and Eve were ashamed

Adam and Eve

THE GARDEN OF EDEN

Adam and Eve lived in the Garden of Eden, which was a beautiful place. The word 'Eden' sounds like the Hebrew word 'delight'. Eden was probably the land between the Tigris and Euphrates rivers, and the Garden, or park, was in the east.

GARDENERS

God put Adam and Eve in charge of looking after the Garden and all the animals.

God told them that they could eat from every tree in the Garden, except one. They must not eat fruit from the Tree of Knowledge (of good and evil), or they would die.

THE SERPENT

The Devil pretended to be a serpent, or snake. Slithering up to Eve, he told her that if she ate the forbidden fruit, she would be 'like God', knowing good and evil. Tempted by the fruit and greedy for more power, Eve ate some. Then she gave fruit to Adam to eat too.

THE FALL

When they had eaten the fruit, Adam and Eve realized for the first time that they were naked, and they were ashamed. They stitched fig leaves together to make loincloths. When God came to the Garden, Adam and Eve hid. God saw that they had eaten from the Tree of Knowledge, and he threw them out of the Garden. They had 'fallen' from being perfect.

Bible Search

- Creation of Adam and Eve: *Genesis 2*
- The fall: *Genesis 3*

CAIN AND ABEL

The story of Adam and Eve shows how sin first came into the world, when they disobeyed God and ate the forbidden fruit. The story of their children, Cain and Abel, shows that sin was passed on. It became natural.

Cain was a farmer

Abel was a shepherd

Bible Search

- The story of Cain and Abel: *Genesis 4:1–17*
- The way of Cain: *1 John 3:12*
- The way of Abel: *Hebrews 11:4*

MURDER: THE MOTIVE

Cain was a farmer, and his younger brother Abel was a shepherd. One day they both made offerings to God. Cain gave some of his crops, and Abel killed some of his finest lambs. God was pleased with Abel's offering, but took no notice of Cain's gift. Abel had given God the best, but Cain probably gave something he didn't really need. Cain was jealous.

Cain's offering

THE CRIME

Cain said to Abel, 'Let's go out to the fields.' While they were there, Cain attacked and murdered Abel. Cain did not murder his brother in a sudden fit of anger (which is bad enough) but planned his revenge.

Cain leaves home

ON TRIAL

When God asked Cain where Abel was, Cain lied and said he didn't know. He was insolent and said, 'Am I my brother's keeper?' But God knew that Cain had murdered his brother. He told Cain his punishment was that he could no longer be a farmer. Nothing that he planted would grow. Instead, he had to leave home and live as a tramp.

Cain was filled with self-pity. He told God the punishment was heavier than he could bear, and that anyone who met him could kill him.

God put a 'mark' on Cain to stop people killing him. We are not told what this mark was.

NOAH AND THE FLOOD

T he descendants of Adam and Eve lived all over the world. But God saw that the people had become wicked, and he decided to destroy every human being and living creature he had created. Only one man and his family were good: the man was Noah.

THE ARK

God told Noah to build a great ship, or ark. The ship was made of cypress wood. It was covered with pitch inside and out to make it waterproof. There were three decks, which were divided off into small rooms. A row of small windows ran round the top of the ship.

WHO WENT INTO THE ARK?

God said that Noah, his wife, their three sons, Shem, Ham and Japheth, and their wives were to get into the ark. They also had to take with them a male and female pair of every kind of animal and bird.

THE FLOOD

When they were all safely in the ark, the rains began. It poured down for forty days, causing a flood so deep that it even covered the mountains. Every living creature was drowned. Finally, the rain stopped and the waters began to go down. The ark came to rest on the Ararat range of mountains in eastern Turkey.

THE RAVEN AND THE DOVE

From the small windows, Noah could only see the mountain peaks and the sky. So he sent out a raven and a dove to see if there was any dry land. The birds saw water everywhere, and flew back. A week later, Noah sent the dove for another look. It came back with an olive leaf. Olive trees do not grow on high land, so Noah knew that the floods must have gone right down. They had been shut up in the ark for 371 days.

THE RAINBOW

God told Noah that he would never again destroy everything in the world by a flood. A rainbow would be a sign to remind people of this promise.

ANY QUESTIONS
1 How deep did the water get during the Flood?
2 Which bird told Noah that the waters had gone down and it was safe to get out of the ark?

Bible Search

- Noah and the flood: *Genesis 6–8*
- The rainbow: *Genesis 9:8–17*
- Noah's faith: *Hebrews 11:7*

BABEL THE TOWER OF

People spoke in different languages

The tower of Babel was never finished. Babel was an ancient city in Babylonia (the country now called Iraq). It is thought that the city of Babylon may have been built on the ruins of the city of Babel.

A TALL TALE

Hundreds of years after the Flood, Noah's descendants were living in the land of Babylonia. Everyone spoke the same language. The people decided to build a city with a tower that touched the sky. They thought it would make them famous. 'If they do that,' said God, 'they will think they can do anything.' So God turned their one language into many different languages. The half-built city became known as Babel, a word which sounded like a Hebrew word meaning 'confused', or 'babble'. Now that nobody knew what anyone else was saying, they couldn't work together and finish building the city. People left Babel and God scattered them throughout the world.

God scattered people throughout the world

STAIRWAYS TO HEAVEN

The tower at Babel was probably an early type of ziggurat. The word 'ziggurat' means 'temple tower'. A ziggurat was a gigantic man-made hill. It had a square base and sides like massive steps. Some ziggurats had five or seven steps, but most had three. Each step was joined to the next by a staircase. Ziggurats were solid, unlike pyramids, and at the top was a small temple.

A ziggurat

Bible Search

- The story of the tower of Babel: *Genesis 11:1–9*

- Building materials: *Genesis 11:3*

- The story of Noah: *Genesis 6, 7, 8, 9*

People left Babel

Traces have been found of over thirty ziggurats, all made from earth and brick. The king of the Babylonians, Nebuchadnezzar, had a ziggurat at Babylon. It was about 92 m (300 ft) square at its base and 92 m (300 ft) high. It had five steps.

11

EMPIRES
SUPER-POWERS IN BIBLE TIMES

When one country becomes powerful, and attacks and conquers many other countries, these become part of its empire. Like a great sea wave, an empire would rise up and control much of the known world for a time: perhaps fifty, a hundred, or maybe a thousand years. Then it would lose its power and another empire would take its place.

EGYPT

Egypt is one of the world's oldest civilizations. Its people were great artists and craftsmen. Egypt was at its most powerful between 3000 BC and 1000 BC.

Moses, the leader of the Israelites, was adopted by an Egyptian princess and grew up in Egypt.

- God in control:
Isaiah 45
- The end of Babylon:
Isaiah 14:22–23

The people of Assyria were fierce warriors

ASSYRIA

Assyria was the northern part of modern Iraq (the land between the River Tigris and River Euphrates). Its capital was Nineveh. The people were fierce warriors, and conquered Israel. Assyrian kings also built beautiful palaces and temples.

The Assyrian empire was greatest from 1400 BC to 1100 BC, and between 911 BC and 609 BC.

BABYLONIA

Babylonia was in the southern part of what is now Iraq. Abraham came from the city of Ur in this area (often called Mesopotamia).

Fifteen hundred years after Abraham's time, the Babylonians conquered Assyria. Later they destroyed Jerusalem. Babylonia was very strong about 1850 BC under King Hammurabi, and also between 612 BC and 539 BC.

PERSIA

Persia is now northwest Iran. King Cyrus II of Persia captured Babylon in 539 BC. He told the Jews they could go back home to Judah. The Persians held their enormous empire for nearly 200 years between 549 BC and 331 BC, until they were conquered by a Greek, King Alexander the Great.

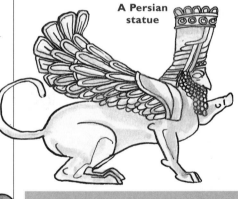

A Persian statue

CANAAN

Canaan was not an empire. It was a small country, but it was important because all trade routes passed through it. The Canaanites became wealthy from trading. Canaan linked three continents: Europe, Asia and Africa, so all the great countries wanted to control it.

ABRAHAM THE FATHER OF THE JEWISH NATION

Abraham

Abraham lived in the city of Ur. One day, God told Abraham to leave Ur and travel far away to the country of Canaan, where he would make him the father of a great nation. Abraham trusted God and decided to do what he said. Abraham set off with his wife, Sarah, and his nephew, Lot. Other relations, servants and animals went too.

MESOPOTAMIA
(now called Iraq)

• Harran

River Euphrates

• Shechem

CANAAN

Ur •

EGYPT

**Ur to Haran
900 km (560 miles)**

**Haran to Canaan
700 km (450 miles)**

River Nile

Red Sea

A PROMISE

Abraham was to become the father, or founder, of the Jewish nation.

God told Abraham, 'You will have as many descendants as stars in the sky.' Abraham was surprised because he and Sarah were very old, and had no children. But soon Sarah did give birth to a son, called Isaac.

Bible Search

- Abraham leaves Ur:
Genesis 12:1–9

- A promise:
Genesis 13:16

- God's test:
Genesis 22:1–18

THE JOURNEY

Abraham and his people travelled for a long time, living in tents. Their first stop in Canaan was Shechem. Here God told Abraham, 'I will give this land to you and your people.'

God stopped Abraham from killing Isaac

ISAAC: A TEST

One day, God told Abraham to kill Isaac as a sacrifice, or offering, to God. It was a test to see if Abraham's faith in God was strong. Abraham was just about to kill his son when God said, 'Stop!'

To find out more about Abraham, turn to the pages on Lot, Isaac and Sarah.

SARAH
HAGAR AND ISHMAEL

S arah was Abraham's wife. Sarah and Abraham lived in Ur, but left to travel to Canaan, when God told them to.

Hagar was Sarah's Egyptian slave, and Ishmael was her son.

EGYPT

Because there was a famine, Sarah and Abraham left Canaan and went to Egypt. Sarah was beautiful, and when the ruler of Egypt, the pharaoh, saw her, he took her into his household. Abraham told a lie. He said Sarah was not his wife, because he thought the pharaoh might kill him. When the pharaoh found out the truth he was disgusted, and sent Abraham and Sarah away.

Sarah

HAGAR

Hagar was Sarah's Egyptian slave.

Sarah had no children so she told Abraham to marry Hagar and have a baby with her. Sarah planned to adopt Hagar's child.

Hagar

THE LAW OF THE LAND

More than 4,000 flat clay bricks covered with writing have been dug up from the ancient city of Nuzi in southern Mesopotamia. These were letters, business deals, contracts and wills. They describe daily life at the time of Abraham. We learn that if a woman could not have a child, she could give her servant to her husband and the servant's child became her own.

ISHMAEL

Hagar called her son Ishmael. Fifteen years later, Isaac, Sarah's son, was born. One day Sarah saw Ishmael making fun of his little brother Isaac. She told Abraham that she didn't want Hagar and Ishmael to live with them any more. Abraham was very sad, but God told him to do what Sarah asked. 'I will look after your son Ishmael,' God said.

Ishmael makes fun of Isaac

SAVED BY THE WELL

Hagar and Ishmael went off into the desert. Eventually they ran out of water, and Hagar thought they would die. But an angel appeared and showed her where there was water. They were saved. Ishmael grew up to be a great desert warrior, and the founder, it is said, of the Arab race.

To find out more, turn to the pages on Abraham and on Isaac.

A desert warrior

Bible Search

• Abraham and Sarah in Egypt: *Genesis 12:10–20*

• Birth of Ishmael: *Genesis 16:1–16*

• Saved by an angel: *Genesis 21:8–21*

ISAAC A BABY FOR SARAH AND ABRAHAM

One day, three strangers arrived at Abraham and Sarah's tent. They brought exciting news for Abraham. Sarah, who was listening, laughed aloud when she heard the strangers say that she would have a baby. 'Whoever heard of such a thing,' she said. 'I'm ninety years old!' When the baby was born, he was called Isaac, which means 'Laughing'.

Sarah, Isaac and Abraham

FARMER ISAAC

When famine came, people moved to live where they could find food. But God told Isaac, 'Don't leave this land. I will look after you.' Isaac became a rich farmer and lived a very different life than his father. Abraham had been a travelling nomad.

A MAN OF PEACE

Abimelech, the local chief, was jealous of Isaac. Again and again his men blocked up Isaac's wells. Isaac dug new wells in new areas. Each time, God blessed him. Wells were very important because there wasn't much rain to provide water.

A well

One day, Abimelech rode up with his army general. But he came to make peace, not war. Abimelech had realized that God was on Isaac's side. Isaac and Abimelech celebrated their peace treaty with a feast.

Isaac became a farmer

Bible Search

- Isaac's birth:
Genesis 21:1-6

- A peace treaty:
Genesis 26:26-31

- Isaac meets Rebekah:
Genesis 24:62-67

A feast

REBEKAH: AN ARRANGED MARRIAGE

It was important to find the right wife for Isaac, because Isaac's family were to be part of God's plan for the world. Rebekah was God's choice. (To find out how Rebekah was found, turn to the page on Esau.) Rebekah put on a long veil when she first saw Isaac. This was a sign that she was not married.

ESAU AND JACOB

Sadness came to Isaac from inside his own family. Isaac and Rebekah had twin sons, Esau and Jacob. But the sons were rivals, not friends. To find out what happened, look up the page on Esau.

LOT, SODOM AND GOMORRAH

Lot grew up in the beautiful city of Ur. God told his uncle Abraham to leave Ur and travel to Canaan. Lot went with him, and so did other members of the family and all their servants. They lived a nomadic life, moving from place to place, and living in tents.

SODOM

Lot drifted to the plains south of the Dead Sea. He settled in a town called Sodom, near to a town called Gomorrah. The people of Sodom were very wicked, and God decided to destroy the city. He sent two angels to rescue Lot and his family. They led them out of the city and told them to hurry away without looking back. But Lot's wife turned to look at the city. She instantly became a pillar of salt.

WHAT HAPPENED?

Sodom was probably destroyed in a great volcanic eruption. Boiling tar and minerals rained down on the city. The quaking, shaking land may have dropped slightly, and the waters of the Dead Sea overflowed into nearby cities.

Lot's wife looks back

Lot

ABRAHAM AND LOT SEPARATE

Both Lot and Abraham had flocks of sheep and goats, and many servants. At the place in Canaan where they decided to settle, there wasn't enough good land and water for everyone. 'We must not fight,' Abraham said. 'Choose where you want to live.' Lot decided to go eastwards.

FACT OR FICTION?

Today, there is no trace of Sodom. Did it ever exist? In 1975, archaeologists working hundreds of miles away found 20,000 flat clay bricks covered with writing. And on some of those old bricks, dating from 2400 BC, are the names of cities ruled over by the kings of Ebla. Among the names are Sodom and Gomorrah.

Bible Search

- Lot's choice: **Genesis 13**
- Abraham prays for Sodom: **Genesis 18:16–33**
- Lot escapes: **Genesis: 19:15–29**

ESAU

Esau the hunter

[E]sau and Jacob were the twin sons of Rebekah and Isaac, and the grandsons of Abraham. Abraham and his family had settled in Canaan. But when Abraham's son, Isaac, was old enough to get married, Abraham decided that his wife should come from the country where Abraham was born: Mesopotamia.

ELIEZER'S CAMELS

Abraham sent his servant, Eliezer, to Mesopotamia. He took with him ten camels loaded with presents. Eliezer arrived at the city of Nahor and sat down to watch women drawing water from a well. He prayed: 'I'll ask one of the girls for water. If she gives me a drink and also offers to water my camels, let this be a sign that she is the wife for Isaac.'

REBEKAH

Eliezer saw Rebekah approaching the well. When Eliezer asked her for a drink, she offered to water the camels too. She was the one!

Eliezer explained why he had come to Rebekah and her family. Rebekah was brave, and agreed to go to Canaan and marry Isaac.

ESAU AND JACOB

Rebekah and Isaac had twin sons: Esau and Jacob. As the elder son, Esau had special rights called his birthright. A birthright was the right to be the head of the family when the father died. In this case, it also meant the right to inherit God's promises to Abraham and Isaac. In time, Esau would take over as the leader of the people.

One day, Esau was hungry, and asked Jacob for some soup. Jacob said he would give him some – for a price. The price was that Esau should give up his birthright to Jacob. Esau agreed.

Brave Rebekah

Rebekah's stew

A BLESSING BY DISGUISE

Isaac was old, blind and close to death. He sent Esau out to kill a deer and make his favourite meal. Isaac planned to bless Esau after he had eaten. Rebekah overheard. She wanted Jacob to receive his father's blessing, not Esau. She quickly cooked a stew. Then she dressed Jacob in his brother's clothes and put goatskins on his hands and neck so that he felt hairy like Esau. The trick worked. Jacob got Esau's dying blessing. Giving a blessing before you died was like making a will.

Isaac and Jacob

- Eliezer finds Rebekah: *Genesis 24*

- Daddy's pet: *Genesis 25:24–29*

- The birthright: *Genesis 25:29–34*

- The trick: *Genesis 27*

Bible Search

17

JACOB
AND THE NATION OF ISRAEL

The story of Jacob takes up a quarter of the book of Genesis. That shows how important he was. God had promised Jacob's grandfather, Abraham, that he would make his descendants into a great nation. And God passed that promise on to Jacob. God named Jacob 'Israel' and the nation was called after him. His sons were the founders of the twelve tribes of Israel.

Jacob at Haran

BETHEL

Jacob had to leave home after he tricked Esau out of his birthright. (See the page on Esau.) He set off to stay with his uncle at Haran. One night on his journey, Jacob dreamt of a stairway leading to heaven, with angels on it. God appeared at the top of the stairs and told Joseph he would give him the land he slept on. When Joseph woke up, he named the place where he had slept 'Bethel', meaning 'House of God'.

HARAN

Jacob stayed with his uncle Laban, and fell in love with Laban's daughter, Rachel. Laban tricked him into marrying his other daughter, Leah, before he allowed him to marry Rachel too.

Shechem

Bethel

RIVER JABBOQ

On the journey to **Aram** Canaan, Jacob was a worried man. He thought Esau would be waiting to kill him. Jacob stopped for the night at the River Jabboq. Suddenly, a stranger appeared and began to fight Jacob. They fought all night, until dawn. Then the stranger left, telling Jacob he would now be called Israel instead of Jacob. Jacob realized the stranger was God.

River Jabboq

MAHANAIM

Esau came to meet Jacob with 400 men. Esau forgave his brother.

Jacob realized it was God

SHECHEM

Jacob bought land outside this strong walled city. But he had to leave when his sons made war on the local people.

ARAM OF THE TWO RIVERS (NOW SYRIA)

Jacob was a clever shepherd, and soon he increased the numbers of his flocks of sheep and goats.

Laban and his sons were jealous of Jacob. So Joseph, after living with Laban for twenty years, decided to go back to Canaan. He took his family and all his flocks with him.

BETHEL

Jacob and his family made a new start. God promised the country of Canaan to his family for ever.

HEBRON VALLEY

Jacob settled here, but his adventures were not over.

Beersheba, birthplace of Jacob and Esau

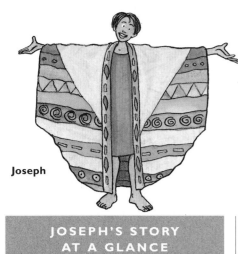

Joseph

JOSEPH
THE COAT OF MANY COLOURS

Joseph was the son of Jacob and Rachel. He had eleven brothers: Reuben, Simeon, Levi, Judah, Issachar, Zebulun, Gad, Asher, Dan, Naphtali, and Benjamin. The family lived in tents in Canaan. Joseph was Jacob's favourite son, so Jacob gave him a beautiful coat made in many different colours. His brothers were very jealous.

JOSEPH'S STORY AT A GLANCE

- Joseph dreamt that he and his brothers were sheaves of corn, and his brothers were all bowing down to him. He told his brothers about the dream. The brothers decided to get rid of him.
- They sold Joseph to traders going to Egypt.
- The traders sold Joseph to be a slave in Egypt. His master's wife fell in love with him. When Joseph refused to fall in love with her, she had him thrown into prison.
- The pharaoh who ruled Egypt had a strange dream. He wanted to know what it meant, but no one could tell him. A man who had been in prison with Joseph remembered that Joseph was good at interpreting dreams. The pharaoh sent for Joseph, who told him that it meant there would be a famine in seven years' time.
- The pharaoh was so impressed that he made Joseph chief minister, with the job of storing up corn before the famine.
- When famine came, Joseph's brothers travelled to Egypt to find food. They went to the chief minister, Joseph, to beg for corn, but didn't recognize him until he made himself known to them. They were amazed!
- Joseph brought his father and all his family to live safely in Egypt.

Joseph's dream

Joseph is sold to traders

Joseph refuses to fall in love with his master's wife

JOSEPH'S COAT

Did Joseph wear a technicolour coat? The Hebrew word for the coat could mean it was brightly coloured, or that it had long flowing sleeves, or that it was beautifully decorated.

THE TRIBES OF ISRAEL

Joseph's brothers became the founders of the twelve tribes of Israel, which were named after them. Joseph's name does not appear because his two sons, Ephraim and Manasseh, each founded a tribe.

Bible Search

- The story of Joseph:
Genesis 37–50
- Joseph's dreams and coat:
Genesis 37:1–11
- Joseph in charge:
Genesis 41:41–43

MOSES THE LEADER

Moses was a great leader. He took a large group of scared slaves and shaped them into an army able to conquer a country. He gave them a code to live by and showed them a God to love.

He had a fiery temper, but became known as the most humble man on Earth, a man who prayed and relied on God.

EGYPT

In the time of Moses, Egypt was at the height of its power. The rulers of Egypt, the pharaohs, made many peoples living in their land into slaves. These included the Israelites, descendants of Joseph.

Slaves carried out most of the work on building sites. To make bricks, water was scooped from a pool and made into a stiff paste with earth. The paste was mixed with chopped straw, and pressed into wooden boxes. The shaped bricks could then be tipped out, stamped with the name of the king, and left to dry in the sun.

A pharaoh

MOSES' CHILDHOOD

You can read about baby Moses on the page on Aaron. Moses was born an Israelite, but was adopted by an Egyptian princess.

Moses grew up in a palace on the Nile Delta. He learned to read and write, and probably studied science, medicine, math and archery.

MOSES IS OUTLAWED

Moses longed to help his own people. One day, Moses killed an Egyptian who was beating a Hebrew slave. Now he had to leave Egypt because his own life was in danger.

He fled to the bleak desert land of Midian. There he became a shepherd, and learned how to live in the desert. Forty years went by.

THE STORY CONTINUES

In Egypt, the Israelite slaves cried out to God to help them. Now turn to the page headed Plagues, to find out more about Moses.

Bible Search

- Slavery in Egypt: *Exodus 1:1–14*
- A humble man: *Numbers 12:3*
- All the wisdom of Egypt: *Acts 7:22*

An Egyptian slavemaster

AARON MIRIAM AND MOSES

A aron was the brother of Miriam and Moses. The family lived in Egypt. Aaron and Miriam helped their brother Moses to lead the Israelite slaves out of Egypt. God chose Aaron to be the first priest of the Israelites. Miriam became a prophet.

A BASKET BOAT

The Israelites were treated as slaves by the Egyptian rulers. When Moses was a tiny baby, the pharaoh (king) ordered that all Israelite baby boys were to be put to death.

The family made a basket boat, put Moses in it, and hid it in the reeds by the River Nile. Miriam kept watch.

The pharaoh's daughter found the baby when she went to the river to bathe. Miriam left her hiding place and offered to find someone to look after the baby. The princess agreed and Miriam fetched her mother.

Moses was adopted by the princess, but thanks to Miriam's quick thinking, he was looked after by his own mother. (Find out more on the page on Moses.)

ANY QUESTIONS
1 Why did the pharaoh order all Israelite baby boys to be put to death?
2 Why was Moses furious when he found the golden calf?

Moses goes up Mount Sinai

THE GIFT OF GAB

One day, when Moses was grown up, God told him to rally the people and rescue them from the pharaoh's clutches. Moses was almost dumbstruck. 'But Lord, I get tongue-tied,' he said.

God said, 'Aaron is a good speaker.' Aaron became Moses' spokesman. Whenever Moses went to the people or to the pharaoh, Aaron was at his side.

God made Aaron the High Priest, or chief priest, of the Israelites.

Moses is found by the princess

UP THE MOUNTAIN

Eventually, Moses led the Israelites out of Egypt. They set up camp in the Sinai desert. Moses went up to the top of Mount Sinai to talk to God. He was gone for a long time, and the people said to Aaron, 'Moses has gone. Make us a god to lead us.'

'Bring me your gold jewellery,' Aaron said. He melted it down and made a golden calf. 'Here is your god,' he said. The people danced and celebrated their new god.

Then Moses came back. He was furious.

On another occasion, Miriam and Aaron grew jealous of Moses and spoke against him. Miriam became ill as a result, but Moses prayed for her to be healed, and she was.

- A basket boat: *Exodus 2:1–10*
- The golden calf: *Exodus 32*
- Aaron and Miriam oppose Moses: *Numbers 12*

Bible Search

PLAGUES AND PASSOVER

Hopping frogs

The Israelites lived far away from their own land, in Egypt. They had been made slaves to the Egyptians, and worked in brickyards. An Egyptian scribe wrote: 'The small builder carries mud...He is dirtier than...pigs from treading down his mud. His clothes are stiff with clay.' (See also the pages headed Joseph and Moses.)

An Israelite slave

THE BURNING BUSH

One day, Moses saw a burning bush that kept burning. God spoke out of the bush. He said, 'Bring my people out of Egypt. I will take them to a new land.'

Moses did not like the idea of leading the people. 'I'm no good at public speaking,' he said. 'Your brother Aaron will speak for you,' said God.

Burning bush

GOD VERSUS PHARAOH

Moses kept asking the pharaoh, the ruler of Egypt, to let the Israelite slaves go free, but the pharaoh refused. So God sent ten disasters, or plagues, to warn the pharaoh. But he was proud and greedy. He would not give in to God. The first nine plagues were:

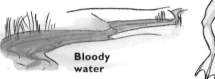

Bloody water

1. All the water in the River Nile turned to blood.
2. Millions of jumping, hopping frogs.
3. Gnats everywhere, crawling on people and animals.
4. Swarms of crawling flies.
5. All the animals died of plague.
6. Boils and sores covered the people.

Boils and sores

7. A massive hailstorm smashed down the crops.
8. The land was black with gobbling, greedy locusts.
9. Total darkness for three days.

Total darkness

Finally came the tenth and most dreadful plague of all. 'The first-born son of every Egyptian will die,' warned Moses. He called the Israelites together and gave them orders:

- Kill a lamb and put its blood on your doorposts.
- Roast the lamb with herbs.
- Make bread quickly without yeast.
- Eat the meal and pack all your things.

That night, the angel of death came to Egypt. But whenever he saw a house with lamb's blood on the doorpost, he passed over the house and no one died. (To find out what happened next, see the page on the Israelites' escape, the Exodus.)

THE PASSOVER

Each spring every Jewish family eats a Passover meal of roast lamb and bread made without yeast. They do this to remember how God acted to set them free.

Bible Search

- Burning bush: *Exodus 3:1–22*
- Jesus eats the Passover meal: *Mark 14:12–26*
- Slaves in the brickyards: *Exodus 1:8–14*

The Egyptian pharaoh

EXODUS THE GREAT ESCAPE

Exodus is the name we give to the Israelites' escape from Egypt, and their long journey to the Promised Land. If there had been no Exodus, there would have been no nation of Israel.

FLIGHT IN THE NIGHT

The Israelites were slaves in Egypt. Moses was their leader. Many times, he asked the pharaoh (king) to set his people free, but the pharaoh refused. So God sent terrible plagues to the Egyptian people. The final, most terrible plague, forced the pharaoh to let the Israelites go free. (See the pages on Plagues and Passover.)

WITHOUT A MAP

God himself led the people; by a pillar of fire during the day, and a pillar of cloud at night. For the first few days, they travelled quickly. Then they came to a sea.

Back in Egypt, building sites and brickyards were silent. There were no longer any Israelite slaves to work in them. The pharaoh changed his mind. 'They're not going to walk out on me!' he shouted. He called up his army, including his war chariots, and they set off in pursuit.

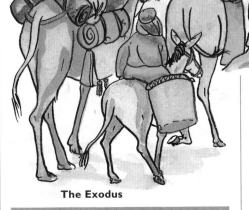
The Exodus

MIRACLE BY THE SEA

The sea that the Israelites had reached is usually said to be the Red Sea. But the Hebrew words in the Bible actually translate as the 'Sea of Reeds'. It may refer to a large stretch of water where the Bitter Lakes are now.

The Israelites looked back and saw clouds of dust: the Egyptian army. They were terrified.

Moses lifted his rod over the water. And an east wind sprang up, driving back the waves, so there was a corridor across the sea bed. Then the people walked across.

STUCK IN THE MUD

The pharaoh and his army raced toward the gap in the water, and on to the sea bed. They tried to catch up to the Israelites, but God caused their chariot wheels to come off. When the last Israelite had reached the opposite shore, Moses stretched out his hand, and the water flowed back. The pharaoh's army was drowned.

ANY QUESTIONS
1 Why did the pharaoh decide to chase after the Israelites?
2 How did God help the Israelites to escape?

The Israelites cross the sea

23

The Israelites camp at the foot of Mount Sinai

SINAI
A MOUNTAIN AND A PACT

T he Israelites' escape from Egypt turned them from a mob of slaves into a nation. They became a people on their way to a land of their own. Events at Mount Sinai turned this people into God's people. They made a pact with God called a covenant. God promised to care for them and they promised to keep his laws.

MOUNT SINAI

In the middle of the rocky Sinai desert, there is a great range of granite mountains. Nothing grows on them. One of these mountains is Mount Sinai (also called Mount Horeb).

God told Moses to bring the people back to worship him at Mount Sinai. The people camped at the foot of the mountain. It was God's holy mountain. No one was allowed to touch it. If they did, they would die. For three days they waited.

FIRE ON THE MOUNTAIN

The mountain began to shake wildly. Lightning flashed. Fire blazed out. A great cloud of black smoke rose and swirled. From the stormy darkness came a sound like a long trumpet blast, growing louder and louder. Moses and Aaron went up the mountain, and there God spoke to them.

Fire blazes out of the mountain

THE TEN COMMANDMENTS

God gave Moses laws for the people to obey. These were the Ten Commandments, written out on two large slabs of stone.

God also gave Moses a long list of rules for living. These were examples of how the Ten Commandments worked in practice. There were rules for how to worship God, how to stay healthy, and how people should live together. Moses wrote these rules down.

Moses wrote down the rules

THE COVENANT

Moses made an agreement, or covenant, with God on Mount Sinai. The people promised to accept God as their ruler and king, and to obey his laws. God promised to look after the people.

To find out more about God's rules for living, turn to the page headed Ten Commandments. To find out more about what happened on the mountain, turn to the page on Aaron.

TABERNACLE
GOD'S TENT

The Tabernacle

The Israelites were camped at the foot of Mount Sinai. God told Moses, the leader of the Israelites, to make a special worship tent (tabernacle is an old word for tent). It was to be a central place to worship God, and to pray in. It would also be used to offer sacrifices to God.

Bible Search

- Building the Tabernacle: *Exodus 35–40*
- The craftsmen: *Exodus 35:30–36*
- God's glory: *Exodus 40:34–35*

THE TABERNACLE

The Tabernacle was about 14 m (45 ft) long, 4 m (13 ft) wide, and 5 m (15 ft) high. Long upright poles were joined by cross poles made of acacia wood covered with gold. Four layers of coverings were stretched over the top, back and sides. The first was decorated linen. Next came a covering made from goats' hair. Rams' skins, which had been dyed red, were put on top of this and then covered with animal skins to make it all waterproof. Four posts covered with gold and draped with a woollen curtain, made a door.

Inner curtains were woven from blue, purple and scarlet linen.

The Tabernacle was surrounded by an open courtyard. In it was an altar made of wood covered with bronze, used for sacrifices, and a great bronze basin for the priests to wash in.

INSIDE THE TABERNACLE

Inside the Tabernacle was the Holy Place, containing a gold-covered altar, a golden lampstand holding seven lamps, and a gold-covered table. Only the priests and their helpers, the Levites, could go in here.

The Ark of the Covenant was a wooden box covered with gold. Inside were the Ten Commandments, Aaron's rod, and a golden jar of manna (special food sent by God). The Ark of the Covenant was kept in a special area known as the Most Holy Place (also called Holy of Holies). Only the High Priest ever went into the Most Holy Place, and then only once a year.

TASK COMPLETED

The Tabernacle took a year to make. It was set up in the middle of the camp. Then a cloud covered the tent, showing that God was there. The beauty of the tent taught the people about the holiness of God.

A priest

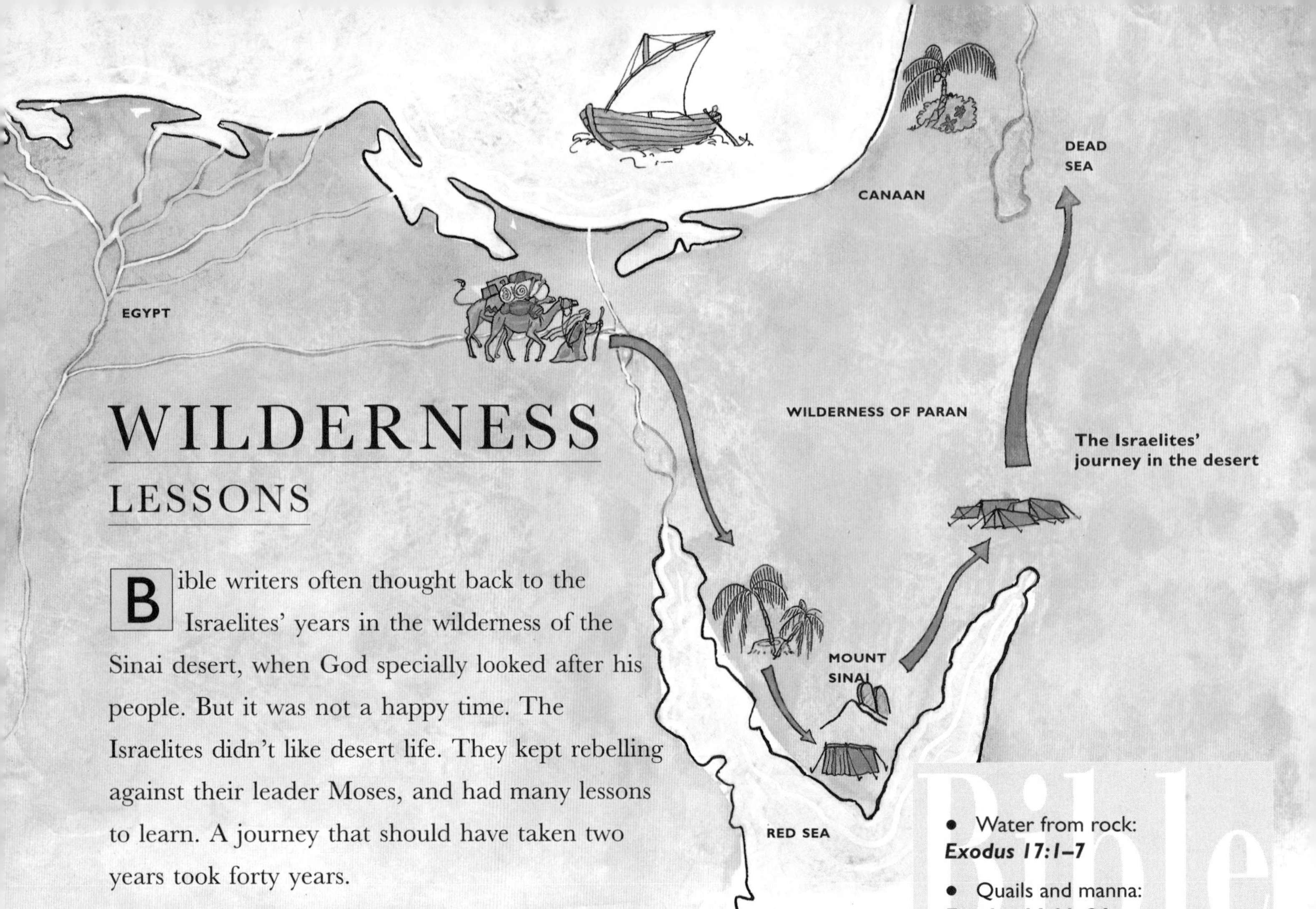

Label text on map:

DEAD SEA

CANAAN

EGYPT

WILDERNESS OF PARAN

The Israelites' journey in the desert

MOUNT SINAI

RED SEA

WILDERNESS
LESSONS

Bible writers often thought back to the Israelites' years in the wilderness of the Sinai desert, when God specially looked after his people. But it was not a happy time. The Israelites didn't like desert life. They kept rebelling against their leader Moses, and had many lessons to learn. A journey that should have taken two years took forty years.

DESERT DIARY

- Journey to Sinai (3 months).
- At Mount Sinai to get God's Law and build the Tabernacle (12 months).
- Journey towards the Promised Land of Canaan (about 8 months).
- A wait at Kadesh, while some of the Israelites go ahead to spy out how the land lies in Canaan (about 40 days).
- The spies report that there are strong cities in Canaan. 'We'd rather die in the desert,' the people moan.
- Waiting. The slaves grow old and die in the desert (38 years).
- Finally, their grown-up children march into Canaan.

MEALS FROM ON HIGH

After five weeks in the desert, the Israelites were starving. 'God will make food rain down from heaven,' Moses replied. Probably no one believed him, but flocks of quails appeared, which the people caught and ate.

The next morning, the people found little, white, sweet-tasting flakes of food lying on the ground. They called it manna, which meant 'What is it?' They ate this every day.

All the water came from water-holes. When they dried up, there was panic. At Massah, God told Moses to hit a rock with his rod, and water flowed out.

Bible Search

- Water from rock: *Exodus 17:1–7*
- Quails and manna: *Exodus 16:11–36*
- Spies go out: *Numbers 13*
- Moses dies: *Deuteronomy 34*

MOSES DIES

After forty years in the desert, Moses knew that he would soon die. He told Joshua that he would have to lead the Israelites into Canaan instead. Then Moses climbed to the top of a mountain, and God showed him the green and beautiful land of Canaan. Moses died on the mountain, his work done. (See the page on Joshua.)

Quail

JOSHUA AND THE LAND OF CANAAN

J oshua's name meant 'The Lord Saves', and that sums up his exciting life. He was a slave in Egypt, until Moses led him and the Israelites to freedom. He became the commander of the Israelites' desert army, and Moses' assistant. God chose Joshua to lead the invasion into Canaan. He was a brilliant army commander, and a man who trusted God.

Bible Search

- Desert warrior:
Exodus 17:8–14
- The spies:
Numbers 13
- God's promise to Joshua:
Joshua 1:1–9
- Shechem:
Joshua 24

SPIES!

From their desert camp, twelve Israelites went to see what the new land of Canaan was like. Ten of the spies said, 'It's a great land! But you should see the people. They're giants. And they live in strong cities.'

The other two spies were Joshua and Caleb. They said, 'Don't be afraid. We'll make mincemeat of them: we have God with us.'

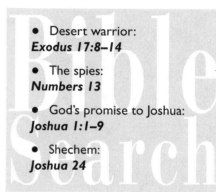

The Canaanites were wealthy

CANAAN

Canaan was the Promised Land, the land God had given to Abraham for the Israelites to live in hundreds of years before.

There were many strong, walled cities in Canaan, ruled over by different kings. The kings often fought each other. It didn't occur to them that it would be a better idea to gang up together to fight the invading Israelite army.

The Canaanite people had become wealthy by trading with other countries. They had comfortable homes, fine furniture, and gold jewellery.

The Canaanites gave the world one very big present: they invented a simple alphabet.

'They're giants,' say the spies

THE RELIGION OF CANAAN

The chief Canaanite god was Hadad, known as Baal (meaning Lord). He was the god of storms and weather. There was also a female god called Asherah.

When the Israelites finally came to live in Canaan, the Canaanite religion proved to be one of the biggest problems they faced. Many Israelites were persuaded that they should worship Baal instead of God.

JOSHUA'S FAITH

Joshua called everyone to a great meeting at Shechem, his capital city. He asked them to make a choice between Baal and God. All the Israelites made an agreement (called a covenant) to serve God.

GIDEON
BEATS THE ENEMY

The story of Gideon is the story of how a young man learned to trust God. He started off as a poor farmer, and ended up a hero. It all began when an angel came to Gideon and said, 'God is with you, mighty warrior. He's chosen you to save your people from their enemies.' At first, Gideon thought God had made a big mistake!

Midianite raiders

A MISSION

For seven years, the Israelites were bullied by Midianite raiders from the desert. The Midianites would ride in on camels and steal crops and cattle, while the Israelites were forced to hide in caves.

The Israelites had begun to worship the Canaanite god Baal, but in the end they prayed to God to come to their rescue.

- Gideon's story:
Judges 6 and 7
- The beginning:
Judges 6:11–24
- Wet wool:
Judges 6:36–40
- A smashing success:
Judges 7

GOD CALLS GIDEON

One day, an angel came to Gideon and told him that God wanted him to save the Israelites from the Midianites. The first thing Gideon had to do was to get rid of the idol of Baal which the people had been worshipping. He did it in the night when no one could see him!

Gideon's second mission was to fight the Midianite army and drive them away. There were thousands of Midianites, and Gideon had only 300 men on his side. How could Gideon win?

Gideon gets rid of Baal

A SMASHING SUCCESS

Gideon gave each of his soldiers a sword, a trumpet and a smouldering torch hidden in a pottery jar. In the dead of night, they surrounded the enemy. When Gideon blew his trumpet, his men blew their trumpets, broke the jars and waved the flaming torches in the air. They yelled out, 'For the Lord and for Gideon!'

Gideon blows his trumpet

The Midianites were terrified and ran for their lives. They thought they were surrounded by a great army!

Now the Israelites no longer had to live in fear. For the next forty years, Gideon ruled over the people in peace.

JUDGES
THE LEADERS OF THE PEOPLE

The Book of Judges is a story of heroes, cowards and traitors. The cowards and traitors were the Israelite people. They were traitors to God, who had loved them and looked after them. The heroes were the judges.

JUDGES

A judge was a cross between a sheriff from the American wild west, a tribal warrior chief and a preacher. The Book of Judges gives the names of twelve judges. They ruled over tribal districts, not over the whole country, but sometimes God called them to deliver the nation from its enemies.

EHUD

Ehud was left-handed. He hid his sword on the inside of his right leg, and pulled it out with his left hand. This tactic caught his enemy by surprise.

Ehud

DEBORAH

Deborah would sit under a palm tree, and people came to her for advice.

The Israelites' enemy, King Jabin, had 900 iron chariots. 'Go and fight Jabin,' Deborah said to Barak. 'I daren't,' he said. 'I'll only go if you go with me.' 'God has given the enemy to you,' Deborah said.

So Barak and his troops waited on a mountain. Sisera, King Jabin's army commander, and his chariots were in the valley below. God sent a heavy rainstorm. The River Kishon flooded, making the chariots useless, and the army was routed.

Deborah tells Barak to fight Jabin

SAMSON THE STRONG

Samson was a fierce fighter. He killed a hungry lion with his bare hands. His story shows that even heroes were sometimes bad. (Look at the page on Samson to find out his story.)

Samson fights a lion

Bible Search

- Deborah's victory song: **Judges 5**
- Lawless days: **Judges 21:25**
- Samson the strong: **Judges 13–16**

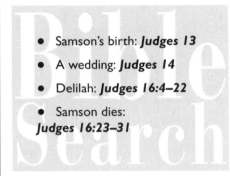

Delilah cuts
Samson's hair

Bible Search

- Samson's birth: *Judges 13*
- A wedding: *Judges 14*
- Delilah: *Judges 16:4–22*
- Samson dies: *Judges 16:23–31*

SAMSON
A VERY STRONG MAN

Samson grew up in Zorah. Around Zorah, the Israelites had given in to the Philistine enemy. Samson was a rebel who never gave in. He fought a one-man battle with the massive strength that God had given him. But he was weak in other ways, and cared more about himself than about God.

Samson was a judge. Judges ruled over tribal districts.

SAMSON'S MOTHER

An angel told Manoah's childless wife that she would give birth to Samson. 'Your baby is to be a Nazirite,' said the angel. A Nazirite was someone who promised to work only for God; sometimes for a short time, sometimes for life. As a sign of this promise, a Nazirite never cut his hair.

SLIPPERY SAMSON

The Philistines were Samson's sworn enemy. But every time they thought they had caught Samson, he escaped. Once, they locked the gates of a city, but Samson tore up the gates and the gateposts, and walked out. Their only hope was trickery.

Samson

DELILAH

Samson fell in love with Delilah. The Philistine chiefs told Deilah that if she found out what made Samson so strong, they would give her a lot of money.

So Delilah kept asking Samson to tell her his secret. 'It's my long hair,' he said at last. When he was asleep, Delilah cut off his hair. All Samson's strength left him, and he was seized by the Philistines.

Samson pulls a millstone

SAMSON DIES

The Philistines blinded Samson and set him to work pulling a millstone to grind corn. One day, all the Philistine leaders met together in their temple. 'Let's have some fun,' they said. They brought Samson out. His hair had grown again. 'Lord, give me strength once more,' Samson prayed. He felt for the pillars holding up the building and pushed hard. Down crashed the temple, killing all the Philistines, and killing Samson, too.

You can read more about the Philistines on the page on Samuel.

30

SAMUEL A GREAT JUDGE

Samuel was the last and greatest of the judges, and one of the first prophets. Judges governed Israel before it had a king. He was a hero, not just in his own area, but to the whole country. He led the people back from idol worship to God. Thanks to Samuel, the Israelites beat the Philistines.

Samuel

HARD TIMES

Samuel was born after his mother prayed for a baby. To find out how God called him, turn to the page on Children.

The Ark of the Covenant

When Samuel was young, there was a terrible battle. The Philistines captured the Ark of the Covenant (a holy box containing God's laws). The Ark was very important as it was a sign to the people that God was with them. The loss of the Ark left the Israelites at rock bottom.

IRON

Iron weapons were made by smelting iron ore in very hot furnaces. The Philistines first brought this skill to Canaan. Before then, 'iron' chariots were wooden chariots studded with small lumps of iron. The Philistines sold iron tools to the Israelites, but not iron weapons.

PHILISTINES

The Philistines came from across the sea, from the country of Crete. They settled along the coast, in five cities ruled by five tyrant kings. One secret of Philistine power was that they knew how to make iron weapons, whereas nobody else did. Another secret was that the kings joined together to fight, which made them very powerful. In the time of Samuel, the Philistines wanted to take over the whole of Canaan.

A Philistine ship

KING-MAKER

Samuel's work was mainly to settle disputes between people. He also led their worship of God, and directed the army.

When Samuel was old, the people were afraid. Who would lead them when Samuel was dead? God told Samuel to anoint first Saul, and later the shepherd boy David, as king. (See the pages on Saul and David.)

Bible Search

- The great defeat: *I Samuel 4*
- Iron: *I Samuel 13:19–21*
- Samuel's regular work: *I Samuel 7:15–17*
- Victory: *I Samuel 7*

SAUL AND JONATHAN

Saul was the first king of Israel. His story is one of the saddest in the Bible.

God told Samuel to find a king to rule Israel. When Saul came to the city where Samuel lived, God told Samuel to make Saul king.

GOD'S CHOICE

Saul was young, handsome and taller than anyone else.

Saul was looking for his lost donkeys when he met Samuel. Samuel told Saul that he was to be the first king of Israel.

When Samuel came to make Saul king, Saul had disappeared. Eventually he was found hiding among some baggage. Samuel anointed Saul by pouring oil on Saul's head. That was how a king was crowned.

Samuel anoints Saul with oil

Saul hides among some baggage

A WAR CHIEF

Spears

Men from the tribes of Israel gathered together into a small army, led by Saul. They won some victories, but Saul had two big faults: he looked at his problems instead of at God; and he got big-headed.

Weapons of war

SAUL IN A MESS

A few years after Saul had become king, the Israelites were about to be attacked by the Philistines. Samuel told Saul to wait for him to make an offering to God, before the battle started. But, scared of the enemy, and in a panic, Saul did not wait for Samuel to offer sacrifices. He did it himself.

Samuel told Saul that he had disobeyed God's word, and that his descendants would not now rule Israel. Saul felt crushed. He began to have fits of misery and madness. (Read more about Saul on the page on David.)

JONATHAN

Jonathan was Saul's son. He was a brave warrior and a devoted friend to David, who became king after Saul.

DEATH ON THE HILL

All Saul's sons died in a terrible battle on Mount Gilboa. Saul was very seriously wounded too, and killed himself.

- Saul is made king:
1 Samuel 10

- God leaves Saul:
Samuel 15

- Jonathan and David:
1 Samuel 18:1; 20

- David's sad poem:
2 Samuel 1

Bible Search

While David was out in the fields, Samuel visited his seven brothers

DAVID THE FAMOUS KING

More stories have been written about David than about any other person in the Bible, except Jesus. David was the greatest king his country had. He made the army strong, and beat the Philistines. He reorganized the government of the country. He also organized the worship of God.

AT THE PALACE

David joined King Saul's staff as an armour carrier.

Sometimes he played the harp for Saul, to calm him when he was in a bad mood. David became close friends with Saul's son Jonathan, and married Michal, Saul's daughter. David was the best fighter in Saul's army. Saul began to grow jealous.

MICHAL

Michal realized David's life was in danger. She helped David to escape through a window. Then she put a statue in the bed, covered it with a sheet, and put goat's hair over its head.

That night, Saul sent his men to fetch David. Michal told them that David was ill. When the men saw what they thought was David, in bed, they went away.

Michal put a statue in David's bed

OUTLAW

David hid in the rocky desert with his men. Once, Saul and his soldiers stopped at the cave where David was hiding. They did not see David, and David had the chance to kill Saul.

When Saul left the cave, David shouted after him that he had just spared Saul, when he could have killed him. Saul realized that David was a great man.

Read more about David on the page on Queens.

- David's song of praise: *1 Chronicles 29:10–13*

- Kindness to Saul's son: *2 Samuel 9*

- David anointed king: *1 Samuel 16:1–13*

- A good king: *2 Samuel 8:15*

A SHEPHERD

David had seven elder brothers. God told Samuel that he had chosen one boy in the family to be the next king. So, one day Samuel went to Bethlehem to visit the brothers. David was still out in the fields with the sheep. Nobody thought he was important enough to meet Samuel.

God told Samuel that none of the brothers he had met was to be king. So Samuel asked to see David.

David was God's choice. Samuel anointed him and told the family that David would be the next king of Israel after Saul.

SOLOMON A WISE MAN

S olomon was the son of King David and Queen Bathsheba. He was the third king of Israel. One night, in a dream, God offered him anything he wanted. He asked for wisdom. In later years, people looked back to his reign as a golden age. Solomon was a clever ruler, and brought wealth and power to Israel by trade and by marrying into the ruling families of other countries.

Trading with other countries

THE TEMPLE

Solomon built the first Temple. It was a magnificent building: 'a glory of gold'. Everyone was proud of it. It was not big: 27 m (90 ft) long, 9 m (30 ft) wide and 14 m (45 ft) high. It was a house for God, not a cathedral for people.

Solomon's Temple

THE KINGDOM

In Solomon's time, the great empires of the world were weak. He made the most of this, and Israel became very rich. Solomon did not gain power by fighting, but by trade, and by marrying the daughters and sisters of other kings.

There were no wars, but Solomon was not popular. He kept his wealth for himself and his friends. He charged heavy taxes and made the people work hard without pay to build his sumptuous palaces, the Temple and other buildings.

TRADING

Camel trains were like our long-distance trucks. Solomon made camel trains from other countries pay when they passed through his land.

For the first time, Israel had a navy. Solomon's ships brought back gold, silver, jewels, ivory, expensive wood, baboons and other animals. Ships did not have to go through other people's lands and pay taxes!

Solomon built up an army of chariots to guard against attack. His 1,400 chariots were kept in six frontier 'chariot cities'.

WISE MAN

Solomon wrote 3,000 proverbs and 1,000 songs. His wisdom was the talk of the world. But he misused God's gift of wisdom. He studied 'everything under the heavens', but he slowly forgot God. He began to worship the same idols as his 700 wives and 300 mistresses.

God said to Solomon: 'You have not obeyed my commands. So I will tear your kingdom away from you.'

Bible Search

- Solomon asks for wisdom:
  I Kings 3:1–15
- Silver in Jerusalem:
  I Kings 10:27
- The Queen of Sheba's verdict:
  I Kings 10:1–13

The people paid heavy taxes

QUEENS
POWERFUL WOMEN

Kings and queens were powerful people. In the Bible, some well-known queens used their power for evil ends.

Jezebel tried to make the people of Israel worship Baal. Herodias had John the Baptist killed.

Jezebel

BATHSHEBA

King David fell in love with a beautiful woman called Bathsheba, but she was already married to an army general. David gave orders for Bathsheba's husband, Uriah, to be sent to the front line, hoping he would be killed in battle. Uriah was indeed killed in the next battle, and so David made Bathsheba his queen. But David had done wrong in God's eyes.

Bathsheba and David had a son called Solomon. When David was old, Solomon's half-brother Adonijah plotted to seize the throne. Just in time, Bathsheba found out and told David. At once, David made Solomon king.

JEZEBEL

King Ahab of Israel married Princess Jezebel of Tyre. The new Queen Jezebel worshipped the god Baal, and she tried to make this the only religion in Israel. But the prophet Elijah stood up to her, and the Jewish religion survived.

Jezebel came to a gruesome end: her enemies threw her from an upstairs window to a courtyard below.

QUEEN OF SHEBA

The Queen of Sheba came from Arabia to see King Solomon. She brought gifts of gold, jewels and spices. She may have come on a trading mission, but her visit turned out to be more than a business trip. When she saw how wise Solomon was, she praised Solomon's God.

The Queen of Sheba

HERODIAS

Strictly speaking, Herodias was not a queen. Her second husband, Herod Antipas, was a 'tetrarch', ruling Galilee for the Romans. But everyone called him King.

'Herodias is breaking the law of Moses,' John the Baptist thundered. 'She has left one husband and married his brother.' Herodias had John thrown into prison.

Herodias' daughter, Salome, danced for Herod at his birthday party. As a reward, he promised her anything she wanted. 'Ask for John the Baptist's head on a plate!' said Herodias. John was beheaded in prison.

Salome

- Bathsheba:
2 Samuel 11; 1 Kings 1

- Queen of Sheba:
1 Kings 10:1–10

- Herodias:
Matthew 14:1–12

Bible Search

ELIJAH A GREAT PROPHET

Jezebel sent a slave to kill Elijah

Elijah was one of the great prophets of Israel. He saved his country from a takeover by the priests of the Canaanite god Baal. Elijah came from Tishbe, on the edge of the desert.

Queen Jezebel, wife of King Ahab of Israel, wanted to make Baal the only god in Israel. She decided to kill every prophet of God that she could find.

A SHOWDOWN

'There will be no rain until I say so,' Elijah told Ahab. Slowly, the grass turned brown. The harvest failed.

Three years passed. Elijah told Ahab to summon the leaders of Israel, and 850 priests of Baal and Asherah, to Mount Carmel.

The harvest failed

Elijah told the people they couldn't worship both God and Baal. He said, 'Let the priests of Baal sacrifice a bull. I will do the same. The God who sends fire to his sacrifice is the true God.'

- Ravens feed Elijah:
  I Kings 17:1–6

- A widow:
  I Kings 17:10–24

- A showdown:
  I Kings 18

- God speaks to Elijah:
  I Kings 19

FIRE

From morning to night, the priests of Baal pranced round their altar. They cut themselves with knives. 'O Baal, answer us,' they shouted. There was no reply.

At the end of the day, Elijah prayed to God. Lightning flashed and burnt up Elijah's sacrifice. 'The Lord is God,' the people cried. The priests of Baal were killed. Then God sent rain to end the drought.

Elijah prepares to sacrifice a bull

MOUNT SINAI

Jezebel was furious when she heard what had happened. 'I will kill Elijah,' she vowed. Elijah had to run for his life. He went to Mount Sinai in the desert.

God sent a mighty wind, and an earth-quake followed by fire. Then silence fell. God asked Elijah why he was there. 'The people of Israel have killed all the other prophets. Now they are after me,' said Elijah.

God sent Elijah back to stir up rebellion and to overthrow Ahab. 'Find Elisha, to be your friend and to help you,' God said.

Read more about King Ahab and Queen Jezebel on the page on Queens.

Elisha watches as Elijah is carried up to heaven

ELISHA THE SUCCESSOR

Elijah was a prophet. He was getting old, and one day God told him that he had chosen someone to take over from him. God instructed Elijah to find a man called Elisha, and take him on as an assistant and future successor.

Elijah found Elisha at work ploughing a field. He gladly agreed to work with Elijah.

ELIJAH VANISHES

Elijah knew that soon God would take him into heaven. He asked Elisha if there was anything he could do for him beforehand.

'Give me a double share of your spirit,' Elisha said. He meant 'May I carry on your work as a prophet after you?'

Suddenly a chariot of fire, drawn by horses, appeared. Elijah was swept into the chariot, and he was carried up to heaven.

A POOR WIDOW

A widow came to Elisha for help. 'My sons are going to be sold as slaves to pay off the money I owe,' she said. 'All I have left is a little olive oil.'

Elisha replied, 'Ask your friends to lend you all their empty jars. Pour your oil into the jars.'

The woman started pouring her oil, and it didn't run out. When the jars were full, the oil stopped flowing. The woman sold the oil and paid off her debts.

A WAR STORY

The king of Aram was at war with the king of Israel. But every time he tried to set up an ambush, the king of Israel found out.

The king of Aram's men told him that Elisha was able to forsee the planned attacks, and warned the king of Israel. So the king of Aram sent his army to capture Elisha.

But Elisha prayed, and the enemy army couldn't recognize him or work out what he was doing. Elisha led them into the city of Samaria. When the men realized what he had done, they found they were trapped.

Elisha told the king of Israel to prepare a feast for the enemy army. When the king of Aram found out what had happened, he never tried to fight the king of Israel again!

Bible Search

- Ploughing:
  1 Kings 19:19–21
- The widow's oil:
  2 Kings 4:1–7
- The blind army:
  2 Kings 6:8–23

The poor widow

KINGDOM OF ISRAEL

When King Solomon died, his kingdom split into two: Judah in the south, and Israel in the north. Israel was the larger and richer of the two countries. That made it a tasty morsel for other countries to grab. Israel only lasted 200 years, before it was destroyed by the Assyrians.

THE SPLIT

When Solomon died, the twelve tribes of Israel had to decide who would be the new king. Solomon had one son, Rehoboam. Rehoboam was made king. Because taxes had been very high under Solomon, and the people had been forced into slave labour, Jeroboam and others asked Rehoboam to make life easier. He promised to make it even harder!

So the kingdom split into two. Ten of the tribes made Jeroboam the king of Israel, and Rehoboam became king of the other two tribes in Judah.

Rehoboam promises to make life even harder

JEROBOAM I

Jeroboam made a fatal mistake. He wanted to stop everyone going off to Jerusalem to worship God. So he built temples at Dan and Bethel, and put a gold statue of a bull in each. Jeroboam may have installed the bulls in God's honour. But the people began to worship the bulls as well as God. That started the rot in the country of Israel.

KINGS

One bad king followed another. Some, especially Omri and Jeroboam II, were strong kings and almost made Israel a world power again. But none gave wholehearted service to God. They worshipped stars, and served the god Baal. Some even sacrificed their own children to these gods. In 200 years, there were nineteen kings.

TEN LOST TRIBES

When the Assyrians conquered Israel, they had a devastating way of stopping future rebellion. They took away part of the population as prisoners of war.

The calamity hadn't come without warning. Over and over again, the prophets had been telling the people that they must turn to God and obey him.

Find out more on the pages headed Elijah and Elisha.

Prisoners of war

- Summing up Israel's kings:
  2 Kings 17:7–23

- The split of the kingdom:
  1 Kings 12

- Red alert:
  Amos 6:4–7; 8:3–4

A bad king sacrifices his child

KINGDOM
OF JUDAH

Read the page on the Kingdom of Israel, first.

When King Solomon died, the tribes of Judah and Benjamin formed the small mountain country of Judah, ruled by Solomon's son Rehoboam.

The people of Judah believed that God wanted David's descendants to be their kings. So each king was followed by his son.

ENEMIES FROM THE OUTSIDE

The country was often at war. Judah's main enemies were:
• Israel and the city state of Damascus, until they were swallowed up by Assyria.
• Assyria. Then Assyria was beaten by Babylonia.
• Babylonia. In 586 BC, Babylonia destroyed Judah.

ENEMIES FROM THE INSIDE

Worship of the Canaanite god Baal was common. On hilltops and in little groves of trees, sacrifices were offered to idols. Some kings were true to God: Asa, Jehoshaphat, Joash, Hezekiah, and Josiah.

HEZEKIAH

When the Assyrian army attacked Jerusalem, King Sennacherib of Assyria wrote, 'I shut King Hezekiah up like a bird in a cage.' But Hezekiah prayed to God for help. The prophet Isaiah said, 'You have trusted God, so God will save you.' A plague swept through the Assyrian army, killing many men. The soldiers who survived packed up and left.

JOSIAH

Josiah was eight when he became king. When he was sixteen, he made up his mind to work for God. He told the priests to mend the broken-down Temple in Jerusalem.

One day, the workmen found an old scroll. It was a lost copy of God's teachings. Josiah called a meeting of all the people and read the book aloud. The people promised God that from now on they would keep his laws. And they did, for as long as Josiah was alive.

To find out about the fall of Jerusalem, see the page on Exile.

Bible Search

• Hezekiah:
Isaiah 37 and 38

• Asa:
2 Chronicles 14; 15

• Josiah:
2 Kings 22 and 23

EXILE

THE FALL OF JERUSALEM

'**W**e're quite safe,' said the people who lived in Jerusalem. 'The Temple is here. God won't let anything happen to his house.' But the prophet Jeremiah wasn't happy with the way people lived. 'Clean up your lives!' Jeremiah warned. 'If you don't, God will bring disaster on you.' Hardly anyone believed him. But Jeremiah was right. In 586 BC, King Nebuchadnezzar burnt Jerusalem to the ground.

The people of Jerusalem felt safe

Jeremiah

COUNTDOWN TO COLLAPSE

627 BC Jeremiah began preaching.
612 BC Babylon became the new world super-power instead of Assyria.
609 BC Jehoiakim became king of Judah. He tried to silence Jeremiah.
605 BC Jehoiakim fought Babylon.
604 BC Nebuchadnezzar, king of Babylon, attacked Jerusalem. He took many people as hostages, to make sure Jehoiakim did what he said.
598 BC Jehoiakim rebelled again.
597 BC King Nebuchadnezzar captured Jerusalem. He made Zedekiah king. All the important people were taken prisoner.
588 BC King Zedekiah rebelled.
587 BC King Nebuchadnezzar surrounded Jerusalem.
586 BC Jerusalem was destroyed.

A BLIND KING

King Zedekiah tried to escape when the Babylonians took over Jerusalem. But he was caught as he was running away. He was blinded and taken prisoner.

The Babylonians took many of the people of Jerusalem back to Babylon as prisoners. Only the lazy, poor and old were left behind in Jerusalem. But even they rebelled! They killed the Babylonian governor and ran away to Egypt, dragging Jeremiah with them.

To find out what happened next, see the page on Exile.

King Zedekiah

DON'T FIGHT

Jeremiah told the people, 'Don't fight the Babylonians. They're sent by God to teach you a lesson.' His enemies called him a traitor and threw him into prison.

But a man called Ebed-Melech pleaded with King Zedekiah for Jeremiah's release, and the king agreed.

To find out more about Jeremiah, see the page on the Book of Jeremiah.

Bible Search

- Jeremiah warns the people: *Jeremiah 7:1–15*
- Attempted murder of Jeremiah: *Jeremiah 38:1–13*

EXILE OF THE JEWS

King Nebuchadnezzar

E xile means not being allowed to live in your own country. When Judah was captured by the Babylonian king, Nebuchadnezzar, many of the people were forced to go and live in Babylonia. At first, their exile was a nightmare come true. Yet some good did come of it, as the people learned important lessons during this time.

BABYLONIA

Babylonia was the low, flat land between the Tigris and Euphrates rivers, which is modern Iraq.

The Jews must have missed their own country. One of the lines of their songs said, 'By the waters of Babylon we sat down and wept… There on the poplars we hung our harps.'

The Jews weren't kept in prison in Babylonia. They settled down in houses near the Kebar canal, in an area called Tel Abib. The Jews probably worked as builders for King Nebuchadnezzar, and had their own land to farm.

King Nebuchadnezzar ruled for forty-three years. He made Babylon into a magnificent city. The Book of Daniel tells the story about how Nebuchadnezzar came to worship God.

A Babylonian building

The exiles meet together

SYNAGOGUES

Led by the prophet Ezekiel, the exiles began to meet together each Sabbath to study their scriptures, to pray and worship God. This was how the first synagogues began. The word 'synagogue' means 'meeting together'.

Ezekiel taught that God was using the exile to teach the people to obey him. The Jews were never again tempted to worship idols.

A LETTER

The prophet Jeremiah sent a letter to the exiles from Jerusalem. He wrote, 'Build houses and settle down...plant gardens. In seventy years' time, God will bring you back. He has plans to prosper you and not to harm you.'

SCRIBES

A group of men made up their minds to study the law of Moses and to obey God in every way. These men carefully copied down the scriptures and collected together many of the old stories and writings. The men were called scribes.

Bible Search

- A letter: *Jeremiah 29:1–24*
- King Nebuchadnezzar: *Daniel 4*
- A meeting: *Ezekiel 8:1*
- A sad song: *Psalm 137*

EXILE
RETURN TO JERUSALEM

During the time the Jews were forced to live in Babylonia, they became settled. Some of them became wealthy. The years went by, and then King Nebuchadnezzar died. After his death, Persia, under King Cyrus, became the new world power. In 539 BC, Persia invaded Babylonia. Cyrus sent all the exiles back to their own countries.

Nehemiah returns

THE CYRUS CYLINDER

The Cyrus cylinder

In the British Museum in London, you can see a clay cylinder. There is writing all round it. It tells what happened when King Cyrus entered Babylon.

Zerubbabel and Joshua lead the exiles

HOME

You would have thought the Jews would have been delighted to return to their own country, but not everybody was. Those who did set off to journey back had many problems.

Bible scholars have different ideas about the order of events when the Jews returned home, but this is what may have happened.

● 537 BC. Sheshbazzar was made governor of Jerusalem and started rebuilding the Temple.

● 525 BC. Zerubbabel (the grandson of the last king) and Joshua the priest returned to Jerusalem with 50,000 of the exiled Jews. They planned to rebuild the Temple. In 516 BC, the Temple was finished. The prophets Haggai and Zechariah encouraged the rebuilding.

● 458 BC. Ezra, the scribe, went back to Jerusalem with more exiles and large sums of money. Ezra's job was to teach God's laws.

● 445 BC. Nehemiah led a group back to Jerusalem. He started rebuilding the city walls, and fifty-two days later, the walls were finished.

● 445 BC. The people made a covenant, or agreement, with God. They promised that they would be God's holy people.

● 433 BC. Nehemiah went back to Babylon. The people began to break their promise to God. The prophet Malachi told them to keep their word to God, but they didn't.

Nehemiah returned to Jerusalem. He was furious, and set about putting everything right.

That's where the Old Testament ends. But it is over 400 years before Jesus comes. What happened in the meantime? See the page on Exile: Waiting for the Messiah.

Ezra returns

EXILE
WAITING FOR THE MESSIAH

When the Jews came back from exile in Babylonia, they made up their minds to live according to God's laws. This decision was to be tested in the years ahead. The time between the ending of the Old Testament and the birth of Jesus is often called 'between the Testaments'. It lasted over 400 years, and during that time, the Jews were ruled by the Persians, the Greeks, themselves, and the Romans.

Bible Search

- Brave people:
Hebrews 11:32–38

- The King will come:
Zechariah 2:10–13; 9:9–11

Judas Maccabeus

WAITING

The new Temple was not very splendid. The country of Judah was tiny and poor. Yet the Old Testament prophets had promised a golden age, and a splendid kingdom. Where was it? Still to come! Many people longed for the Messiah who would lead them to victory and glory.

A Persian

400 YEARS OF RULERS

- *Persian rule.*
Judah was part of the Persian empire. For a while Esther, who was a Jew, was a queen of Persia.

Alexander the Great

- *Greek rule.*
In 331 BC, Alexander the Great conquered Persia. Ten years later he died, and his vast empire was split between his generals.

Many Jews liked Greek rule. But in 168 BC the Greek ruler, Antiochus IV Epiphanes, tried to force the Jews to become Greek and worship Greek gods. He put the statue of Zeus in the Temple and made the people work on the Sabbath. There was a revolt led by Judas Maccabeus, and after bitter fighting, Antiochus gave in.

- *Self-rule.*
Four years later, Judas' family, the Hasmoneans, began to rule the country. The Jews divided into religious groups. Some wanted worldly power; some only wanted to serve God.

- *Roman rule.*
In 63 BC the Romans led by their general, Pompey, captured Jerusalem.

From 37 BC to 4 BC, the Romans let King Herod rule the country as their puppet king. He built many magnificent buildings, and started to rebuild the Temple. But Herod was an evil man.

Eventually, the Romans destroyed Jerusalem in AD 70.

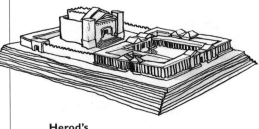

Herod's Temple

GREEKS AND ROMANS

J esus was born in Judea in about 6 BC. By then, Judea (the new name for Judah) was a tiny part of the mighty Roman empire. Roman engineers had built well-paved roads between all the main cities. In this new world there were no language problems: every educated person spoke Greek. (This helped with the spread of the Christian message.)

Educated people spoke Greek

THE GREEKS

About 800 years before the birth of Jesus, self-governing Greek cities grew up along the coast of Greece. From 500 BC–320 BC many brilliant writers, artists and thinkers lived in these cities. Their ideas about science, medicine, architecture, politics, law and freedom, are still important today.

The thinkers Socrates (470–399 BC) and Plato (428–348 BC) lived in Athens. In Athens every citizen had a say in the government of the city: democracy was invented in Greece.

In 334 BC, Alexander the Great set out to conquer the world. His aim was to spread the Greek way of living and thinking.

Plato

ROME

Rome was at first a single, powerful city in Italy. By war and treaties it grew stronger, until Rome ruled Italy. By 156 BC, the Roman armies had made Rome the new world power, conquering other countries to make the Roman empire even bigger than the Greek empire. It contained 54 million people.

The Romans made good rulers. As long as people paid their (often heavy) taxes, and did not rebel, the Romans let them rule themselves and keep their own religions and customs.

GODS

The Greeks worshipped a large number of gods. The Romans took over the Greek gods and gave them Roman names. The chief Greek god, Zeus, was given the Roman name Jupiter.

Zeus

AQUEDUCTS

To bring water to a town, the Romans built bridges that carried water, called aqueducts. Over one million cubic metres (35 million cubic feet) of water a day flowed across the aqueduct outside Rome. It also flowed through underground pipes into thousands of city baths, troughs and fountains.

For more information on Greeks and Romans, see the page titled Exile: waiting for the Messiah.

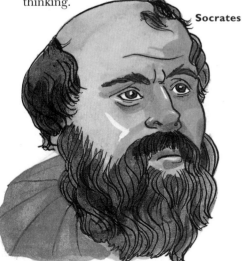

Socrates

The Pont du Gard aqueduct built by the Romans in France

CHILDREN
IN THE BIBLE

In the Bible, children sometimes have important work to do to help God in his plan to rescue the world. Jesus showed children were as important to God as anyone else. He still welcomed them when his older followers wanted them to go off and play.

Jesus loved children

SAMUEL

Hannah and her husband Elkanah were sad. 'Please, Lord, let me have a baby,' Hannah prayed. 'He can work full-time for you when he grows up.'

Samuel's birth was the happiest day of Hannah's life. When Samuel was old enough, Hannah took him to live with old Eli the priest, to help him in his work. One night, Samuel was awakened by a voice. He thought it was Eli, but Eli said he'd been asleep. This happened three more times.

At last, Eli understood that the voice was God, calling Samuel. Eli said, 'If the voice comes again say, "Speak, Lord, your servant is listening." ' Later that night, God gave Samuel a message for Eli. Samuel later became a great leader.

Hannah prays

Samuel is awakened by a voice

A SLAVE GIRL

Naaman and the slave girl

A young Israelite girl who was captured in battle was given to Naaman, the great Syrian general, as a slave. Naaman suffered from leprosy. When the girl saw this, she said, 'In my country there is a prophet called Elisha, who could heal Naaman.'

So Naaman set off for Israel, and went to Elisha's house. The prophet sent out a messenger to tell Naaman: 'Wash seven times in the River Jordan.' Naaman was annoyed that Elisha hadn't spoken to him in person, but he swallowed his pride and went to the river. There he ducked into the water seven times. And God healed him!

After that, Naaman worshipped God.

PAUL'S NEPHEW

When Paul was a prisoner, more than forty Jews swore that they would kill him. Paul's nephew, who was about twelve, heard of their plot. He told Paul, who sent him to see the governor. He was a brave boy, because Paul's enemies were dangerous men.

Paul's nephew overhears the plot

- Children welcomed: *Matthew 19:13–15*
- Samuel: *1 Samuel 1 and 3:1–21*
- Naaman: *2 Kings 5*
- Paul's nephew: *Acts 23:12–22*

Bible Search

NEW TESTAMENT
THE GREATEST STORY
EVER TOLD

The New Testament tells the story of the birth, life and death of Jesus Christ, and the beginning of the Christian Church. These events changed the world.

1 John the Baptist is born

2 Jesus is born

about 6 BC

3 Jesus, Mary and Joseph escape to Egypt

4 The 12-year-old Jesus gets lost in Jerusalem

5 John the Baptist baptizes people in the river Jordan. He also baptizes Jesus

about AD 29

6 Jesus is tempted

7 Jesus calls his disciples

8 John the Baptist is beheaded

9 Jesus spends three years travelling, teaching, healing

10 Jesus enters Jerusalem to waving palm branches

11 Jesus' last week in Jerusalen

12 Jesus' last meal

13 Jesus is crucified

14 Jesus rises from the dead

15 40 days later Jesus returns to heaven

AD 33

16 10 days later the Holy Spirit comes to the disciples

17 Peter preaches the first Christian sermon

18 Stephen is killed: the first martyr

19 To escape attack, and prison, Christians spread out all over the world

AD 34 or 35

20 Saul becomes a Christian

21 The Council of Jerusalem decides anyone can become a Christian without becoming a Jew as well

22 Paul goes on missionary journeys throughout the world and writes letters

AD 46 to 53

23 Paul is in prison in Rome

AD 62 to 64

24 The Book of Revelation is written

25 John, the last disciple, dies

about AD 100

46

PALESTINE
THE HOLY LAND

P alestine is the name of the land Jesus lived in. Bible writers called it 'Canaan', 'The Land of Israel', or 'The Promised Land'. It was the Greeks who named it 'Palestine'. In Jesus' time, Palestine had an amazing variety of scenery: snow-capped mountains, thick forests, and deserts.

In 1948, Palestine was divided and the new country of Israel was formed. This is what we call the country today.

THE COASTAL PLAIN

The coastal plain was about 48 km (30 miles) wide in the south but only a few metres wide in the north. It was a flat area with sand dunes.

The Shephelah was a line of low wooded hills. When the Philistines were attacking from the coast, the Shephelah was a war zone.

CENTRAL HIGHLANDS

In the central highlands, there were three regions: Galilee, Samaria and Judah. Galilee, with its beautiful inland lake, was where Jesus grew up.

The plain of Esdraelon was a flat stretch of land between the hills of Galilee and the hills of Samaria. It was a corridor to the sea used by armies and traders.

Most of the Old Testament stories took place among the high hills and valleys of Samaria and Judah.

THE JORDAN VALLEY

The River Jordan twisted along the deepest valley in the world. The word 'Jordan' means 'descender': a good name, because the river dropped a good distance before it reached the Dead Sea. The valley was a thick jungle where lions roamed.

Across the River Jordan was a vast high plateau, like an uneven table-top. This was the Trans-Jordan plateau. It was very fertile land, with forests and vineyards.

DEAD SEA

The Dead Sea was 77 km (48 miles) long, 16 km (10 miles) wide and 762 m (2,500 ft) below sea-level. It was the lowest place in the world.

There was little rain, and the air was still, heavy and hot. There was nothing but cliffs, rocks and swarms of insects. There was no fish or plant life in the Dead Sea. The water was very salty, felt oily, and smelt of decaying minerals.

JESUS IS GOD

After Jesus died and came back to life again, his friends thought about everything he had said and done. And they became certain that Jesus was God in human form. A writer in the New Testament summed it up when he said, 'The Son reflects the glory of God. He is an exact copy of God's nature.'

Jesus rose from the dead

A REAL HUMAN

Jesus had a human mother, Mary, but he did not have a human father. He was formed in Mary's womb by the power of God's Spirit.

JESUS' ACTIONS SHOW HE IS GOD

Jesus told a storm at sea to calm down, and it did! Jesus' friends knew that only God could control the weather. Jesus said to a man who could not walk, 'Your sins are forgiven...Take your mat and walk.' The man was healed! Everyone knew that only God could forgive sins.

JESUS' WORDS SHOW HE IS GOD

When Jesus said he had seen Abraham, the Jews asked how he could have, as he wasn't old enough. Jesus said, 'I tell you the truth. Before Abraham was born, I am!' In the Old Testament the words 'I am' were God's name for himself.

Jesus said, 'Anyone who has seen me has seen the Father.'

Jesus said, 'The Father and I are one.' When Jesus said this, the Jews tried to stone him. They said, 'You are only a man, but you say you are the same as God.' Stoning was the Jewish way of carrying out the death penalty. It was the punishment for claiming to be God.

A storm at sea

JESUS' FRIENDS REALIZE HE IS GOD

At times, Jesus' friends did not understand Jesus fully. But Peter once realized Jesus was 'the Christ, the son of the living God'. Thomas, the doubter, saw Jesus after he had come back to life and said, 'My Lord and my God.' Later, Paul was to describe Jesus as being the same as God.

Jesus' friends see Jesus is alive again

JESUS' RESURRECTION SHOWS HE IS GOD

Because Jesus was God, he could not die for ever. God the Father brought him back to life, and many people saw him alive.

- Jesus' words:
John 8:58; 14:9; 10:29-31

- Man who could not walk:
Mark 2:1-12

- Storm at sea:
Mark 4:35-41

- Jesus' friends opinion:
Matthew 16:16; John 20:28

Bible Search

JESUS IS BORN

In about the year 5 BC, two people were planning to get married. Their names were Mary and Joseph, and they lived in Nazareth, a town in the hills of Galilee.

One day, something very exciting happened to Mary. The angel Gabriel appeared and said, 'You will give birth to a son. He will be the son of God.'

Joseph

JOSEPH

When Joseph found out that Mary was expecting a baby, he decided to break off their engagement, because he knew he was not the father. But in a dream, an angel told him not to be afraid. 'The baby will be born by the power of God,' said the angel. 'You must call him Jesus (God Saves) because he will save his people from their sins.'

ELIZABETH

Mary went to visit her cousin Elizabeth who lived near Jerusalem. Elizabeth was also expecting a baby. Elizabeth's baby grew up to be John the Baptist.

Mary and Elizabeth

BETHLEHEM

The Roman emperor Augustus Caesar gave orders for a register to be taken of all the people living in the Roman empire. Mary and Joseph had to go to Bethlehem to be registered, which was a three-day journey by donkey.

When they arrived in Bethlehem, the city was full and there was nowhere to stay. That night, Mary gave birth. We know from Luke's Gospel that when Jesus was born, Mary wrapped him in strips of cloth and laid him in a manger. A manger was where animals fed. For this reason, it has always been said that Jesus was born in a stable, probably a cave in the hillside by the inn.

- Gabriel: *Luke 1:26–38*
- Mary and Elizabeth: *Luke 1:39–56*
- Joseph: *Matthew 1:18–25*
- Bethlehem: *Luke 2:1–7*
- Shepherds: *Luke 2:8–20*

SHEPHERDS

On the night Jesus was born, shepherds were guarding their sheep in the hills outside Bethlehem. Suddenly, there was a great light, and an angel appeared. 'Don't be afraid,' the angel said, 'I'm bringing you good news of great joy.' The angel told the shepherds about Jesus.

At once, the shepherds decided to go and visit Jesus, Mary and Joseph.

Joseph and Mary try to find somewhere to stay in Bethlehem

49

JESUS AS A BABY

After Jesus was born, Mary and Joseph moved to a house in Bethlehem. After eight days, Jesus was named and circumcised according to Jewish custom. Forty days later, Mary and Joseph took Jesus to the Temple in Jerusalem, to offer a sacrifice and pray for him to serve God all his life.

Mary and Joseph take Jesus to the temple

WISE MEN

When Jesus was born, a group of wise men saw a new star rising in the east. Their books told them that a new star meant a new king. So they set off for Jerusalem.

The Gospel of Matthew doesn't say the men were kings: it called them 'magi' which meant 'wise men'. They were probably astrologers (men who studied the stars) from Persia or Arabia. We think there were three of them, because they gave three gifts to Jesus.

King Herod, who ruled Judea, was very worried when he heard that a new king had been born. He thought he had a rival for his throne. He sent for the wise men and said, 'Come back and see me when you've found the king.' He wanted to find out where Jesus was.

* In the Temple:
Luke 2:21–38

* Wise men:
Matthew 2:1–12

* Escape:
Matthew 2:13–18

* Return:
Matthew 2:19–23

Bible Search

THE GIFTS

The star led the wise men to the house where Mary and Joseph were living. They gave Jesus gifts of gold, frankincense (a perfumed incense) and myrrh (an expensive scented ointment).

The wise men were warned in a dream not to go back to Jerusalem and see Herod, so they went home a different way.

MURDER

The three wise men

Mary, Jesus and Joseph escape

Herod was furious when the wise men didn't return. So to make sure that the new king didn't survive, he gave orders for all baby boys in Bethlehem under two years old to be killed.

Joseph, Mary and Jesus escaped to live in Egypt. When King Herod died in 4 BC, the family went back to Palestine, and settled in Nazareth.

JESUS GROWS UP

Nazareth

Jesus grew up in Nazareth, a quiet market town in the hills of Galilee. The northern region of Galilee was beautiful, with wooded hills, and many wild flowers. Jews from the south did not like the people of Galilee very much. Galileans spoke with a different accent and many had parents from other countries.

FAMILY

Jesus' father, Joseph, was a carpenter and builder. He would have been an important man in his village, as carpentry was skilled work.

Jesus had at least four younger brothers: James, Joseph, Simon and Judas, and several sisters.

Between the ages of five and thirteen, Jesus went to school in the synagogue in Nazareth. He learnt to read and write and he studied the Bible (our Old Testament).

Joseph and his children

JESUS GOES MISSING

When Jesus was twelve, he went with his family, relatives and friends to the Passover festival in Jerusalem. While they were there, Jesus disappeared. His parents were frantic with worry, but at last they found him, sitting with a class of students in the Temple. Jesus was surprised that they were so upset. He said, 'Didn't you know I would be in my father's house?'

COMING OF AGE

On their thirteenth birthday, Jewish boys were considered to be adults. There was a special service in the synagogue, called the Bar Mitzvah, to celebrate.

Most boys left school at about this age, and went to work with their fathers. A few went on to study in Jerusalem.

HEAD OF THE FAMILY

We think Joseph died when Jesus was a teenager. Mary is always by herself in the Gospel stories. Jesus, as the eldest son, took over his father's business. He was not able to go on to higher education. This is why he was later called 'uneducated'.

Jesus works as a carpenter

Bible Search

- Nazareth: **John 1:46**
- Jesus' family: **Mark 6:1–3**
- No education: **John 7:15**
- Jerusalem: **Luke 2:41–50**
- Growing up: **Luke 2:51–52**

A voice calling
in the desert

Bible Search

- Clothes: *Matthew 3:4*
- His message: *Luke 3:7–14*
- Prison: *Matthew 11:2–19*

JOHN THE BAPTIST

John the Baptist was Jesus' cousin. He was six months older than Jesus. Jesus said that John the Baptist was the greatest prophet there had been, who would get people ready for the coming of God. John said of himself, 'I am a voice of one calling in the desert, "Prepare the way for the Lord."'

JOHN AND KING HEROD

King Herod had married his brother's wife, while his brother was still alive. John told Herod that what he had done was against the law. Herod threw him in prison.

John began to have doubts while he was in prison. He sent a message to Jesus, asking: 'Are you really the one we are expecting?' Jesus assured him he was, by telling him what was happening.

Herod's wife, Herodias, detested John. Turn to the page on Queens to read how she had him beheaded.

ZECHARIAH

Zechariah was an elderly priest. One day, the angel Gabriel came to Zechariah in the Temple and said, 'You will have a son, called John. He will prepare the people for the coming of God.' Zechariah didn't believe the angel, so Gabriel made him unable to speak until John was born. That taught him not to doubt an angel!

Zechariah's wife was called Elizabeth. John was her only child, and she was old when he was born.

Gabriel comes to Zechariah

THE DESERT

When he grew up, John went to live in the desert. He wandered from place to place, preaching to the people. Everybody came to hear him. He said, 'Turn from your evil ways. The Deliverer is coming. I am not fit even to untie his sandals.'

THE BAPTIST

John baptized people when they became Christians. Baptism was a sign that they were sorry for the wrong things they had done. When Jesus came to be baptized, John was surprised. 'You ought to baptize me!' John said.

Many of John's followers left him to follow Jesus, and John was delighted. He said, 'Jesus must become greater and I must become less.'

John in prison

JESUS
IS BAPTIZED AND TESTED

Bethany

J esus was about thirty years old when news reached Nazareth of a new prophet called John the Baptist. He was telling people to turn back to God, and get ready to welcome God's Messiah. He was preaching at Bethany, on the eastern banks of the River Jordan, and baptizing people.

JESUS' BAPTISM

John was shocked when he saw his cousin Jesus coming to be baptized. 'You should baptize me!' John said. Jesus came to be baptized to show he was ready to do what God wanted, and that he was willing to take people's wrongdoing on himself.

People were baptized by dipping their whole body into the water of the lake or river. When Jesus came up out of the water, the Holy Spirit came to him in the form of a dove. And God's voice said, 'You are my son, whom I love; with you I am well pleased.'

Bible Search

- Baptism: *Matthew 3:13–17;*
- Testing: *Matthew 4:1–11; Mark 1:12–13*
- Moses quoted: *Deuteronomy 8:3; 6:16; 13*
- Temptation: *Hebrews 4:15*

John baptizes Jesus

TESTING

After the baptism, the Holy Spirit led Jesus away to the desert wilderness of Judea. There he spent forty days without food, with only the wild animals for company. Then the Devil came to tempt, or test, Jesus.

The Devil asked Jesus to turn stones into bread, to prove he was the son of God, as he claimed. Jesus replied that man could not live on bread alone, but had to find strength from God's words.

Then the Devil transported Jesus to the top of the Temple, and told him to throw himself off. 'If you really are the son of God,' he said, 'you won't come to any harm.' But Jesus said that God was not to be tested in that way.

Finally, the Devil offered Jesus all the kingdoms of the Earth, if he would worship the Devil. Jesus refused, shouting, 'Away from me Satan.' The Devil gave up, defeated, and disappeared.

With these tests, the Devil was trying to tempt Jesus to use his power in wrong ways.

JESUS' DISCIPLES

The word 'disciple' means 'learner'. When Jesus started to preach, people flocked to hear him, and many became his friends and followers. Jesus chose twelve men to be with him all the time, to share his life and his work, and to learn from him. Jesus prayed for a whole night before he finally chose the disciples.

Matthew, also called Levi (left). Matthew was a tax-collector who worked for the Romans.

DISCIPLES AND APOSTLES

After Jesus' death, the disciples became known as apostles. The word 'apostle' meant someone who was sent out as a messenger. The apostles became messengers of the teachings of Jesus.

Andrew (below left). Andrew was a fisherman, and the brother of Simon.

Simon Peter (above right). Simon Peter and Andrew were fishing when Jesus called them to follow him. They were to catch men, instead of fish!

James and John (below). These brothers were also fishermen. Jesus nicknamed them the 'sons of thunder', because they had bad tempers.

Philip (below left). Philip came from the lakeside town of Bethsaida. As soon as Jesus called him, he went off to find his friend Bartholomew.

Bartholomew, also called Nathanael (above right). Jesus told Bartholomew, 'You are a true man of Israel. There is nothing false in you.'

Simon (right). Simon was a zealot. Zealots believed in fighting to get rid of the Romans.

Thomas (right). Thomas is sometimes known as 'Doubting Thomas', because at first he would not believe Jesus had risen from the dead.

James (below). James was the son of Alphaeus.

Thaddeus (above). He was also called Judas, son of James.

Judas Iscariot (below). 'Iscariot' means 'from Kerioth', which was a town in Judea. So if Judas came from Kerioth he was the only southerner in the group of Galileans. He looked after the disciples' money. It was Judas who betrayed Jesus. In the end, he killed himself.

Bible Search

- Andrew, John and Simon:
John 1:35–42

- Fishing:
Mark 1:14–20

- Praying:
Luke 6:12–16

JESUS' FRIENDS

Jesus had many friends about whom we know very little. Luke names three women who probably helped with the shopping, cooking and washing for Jesus and the disciples. One was Mary Magdalene. The others were Joanna, whose husband worked in Herod's court, and Susanna, who we know nothing else about. Mark mentions Salome, too, who was probably the mother of James and John.

Joanna

Susanna

NICODEMUS

Nicodemus was a Pharisee, and a member of the Sanhedrin (a council of religious leaders in Jerusalem). He came to Jesus and said, 'Nobody could do what you do without God's power.' Later, he spoke up for Jesus in the Sanhedrin, and was laughed at.

Nicodemus helped Joseph of Arimathea to bury Jesus' body.

Nicodemus was a member of the Sanhedrin

MARY AND MARTHA

Martha became upset

When Jesus was passing through the village of Bethany, Martha invited him to stay at her house. This meant a lot of work. Martha became upset because while she did all the work, her sister Mary sat listening to Jesus and not helping her.

Very gently, Jesus said to Martha, 'You're worried about many things. Only one thing is necessary. Mary has chosen what is better.' He meant that it was more important to listen to his teaching than to do the housework.

Bible Search

- Nicodemus:
John 3:1–21; 7:50–52
- Martha and Mary:
Luke 10:38–41
- Supporters: *Mark 15:40–41; Luke 8:2–32*

MARY MAGDALENE

Mary Magdalene had done many wrong things, and was very distressed when Jesus met her. She had 'seven evil spirits'. Jesus healed her, and she became one of his closest friends. She was the first person to see Jesus alive, after he was raised from the dead.

Also see the page headed Zacchaeus.

Mary Magdalene

JESUS TEACHES

Jesus opened people's eyes

In the synagogue in Nazareth one day, Jesus was reading aloud: 'The Spirit of the Lord is upon me…to preach good news…to make the blind see…to set prisoners free…' Jesus closed the book. 'Today,' he said, 'these words have come true.' Wherever Jesus went, he opened people's eyes to the truth about God. He did it in many different ways.

THE MESSAGE

Jesus' message to the people was:
• God is a loving father and a great king.
• God's kingdom of love is quite different to the kingdoms of this world.
• Friendship with Jesus is the way into God's kingdom.

TEACHING WITH PARABLES

Jesus taught people by telling stories. We call Jesus' short stories 'parables'. A parable tells a story, but the story also has a special Christian message. For example, this is one of Jesus' parables:

A woman lost a silver coin. She cleaned and swept until she found it. Then she called all her friends, and said, 'Great news. I've found my lost coin.'

The special message in this parable was that people who rebelled against God were like the lost coin, and God was like the woman searching for it.

TEACHING BY ACTIONS

One day, Jesus got a bowl of water and washed his friends' dirty feet. This was a job a slave normally did. 'You must be servants to one another,' Jesus said.

The parable of the woman and the coin

TEACHING BY DISCUSSION

Jesus talked to anyone who came to him. He asked questions, and listened carefully to the replies. He talked to everyone; from Pharisees who thought they knew everything, to the poorest beggar.

TEACHING BY HIS LIFE

Jesus lived without seeking power. He was not greedy. He made friends with all sorts of people. He depended on God. To him, prayer was as natural as breathing. He fought against evil and died for his friends.

Bible Search

• In Nazareth: *Luke 4:16–21*
• Washing feet: *John 13:1–5*
• The lost coin: *Luke 15:8–10*
• Jesus prays: *Mark 1:35*

JESUS HEALS

Jesus made his base in the lakeside town of Capernaum. He travelled all over Galilee, teaching in synagogues and in the open air, and working miracles. Great crowds of people came to see him. Those were exciting, golden days for the disciples.

HEALING

Most of Jesus' miracles were healing miracles. He healed every type of illness, including blindness, fever, leprosy and epilepsy. The Bible tells of three people he brought back from the dead.

Jesus' heart went out to the suffering people he saw. He healed out of love, for he had come to set people free from bad things of every kind. The miracles showed that Jesus was the Messiah the people were waiting for.

HOW JESUS HEALED

Jesus healed in different ways. Sometimes he just commanded, 'Be healed', and sometimes he put his hands on the suffering person. Once, in a great crowd of people, a woman touched the hem of his cloak, and she was healed.

Jesus heals a blind man

Another time, Jesus spat on some dirt to make mud, which he put on the eyes of a blind man making him able to see.

A woman touches the hem of Jesus' cloak

TRUST

Jesus healed people without any fuss; he did not use long prayers, special words, or ceremonies. He simply asked people to trust him. Then he often told them not to talk about it, because he didn't want to be known as a wonder-worker. He wanted people to see the miracles as signs which pointed to truths about God.

FAITH

When Jesus returned to his home town of Nazareth, he could do very few miracles. The people didn't believe that someone who was once the village carpenter could be God's special agent, and Jesus refused to do miracles if people did not trust him.

Some people did not believe Jesus could heal

Bible Search

- Healing: *Mark 1:32–34; 3:7–12*

- A woman in the crowd: *Mark 5:26–29*

- In Nazareth: *Mark 6:1–6*

- Pity: *Matthew 14:14*

- A mudpack: *John 9:6*

Jesus calms the storm

JESUS RULES

Jesus was asleep in a boat on the Sea of Galilee. Suddenly, a violent storm blew up. The disciples woke him. 'We're going to drown!' they shouted. Jesus stood up. 'Silence!' he commanded the storm, and everything went quiet. The disciples were awestruck. They realized that Jesus had power over the Earth.

JESUS FOR KING

One day, Jesus and his disciples went to a quiet area near Bethsaida, to spend time away from the crowds of people who wanted to see him. But the crowds followed him. So Jesus spent the day talking to people, and healing the sick.

Later on, Jesus told the disciples to find food for everybody. There were over 5,000 people! One boy brought Jesus five loaves and two fish. Jesus thanked God for the food, and told the disciples to give it out. Somehow everybody present had enough to eat.

A boy brings loaves and fish

It was another miracle. Excitement rose. Everybody wanted to make Jesus king to lead a rebellion against the Romans, but Jesus sent them all away. After this, many people stopped supporting him.

Everyone had enough to eat

Bible Search

- King of the waves: *Mark 4:35–41*
- King of the loaves: *Mark 6:30–44*
- King of the universe: *Mark 9:2–7*

TURNING POINT

Jesus left Galilee. He visited foreign countries to the east, north and west. He kept clear of crowds and spent his time teaching his friends. 'Who do you think I am?' Jesus asked. 'You're God's special agent,' Peter replied. 'God has shown you this,' Jesus said. 'Don't tell anyone. I must go on to Jerusalem. There I'll be killed and rise again.'

Jesus visited foreign countries

ON MOUNT HERMON

Six days later, Jesus went further north, to Mount Hermon. He took Peter, James and John up the mountain with him. Suddenly, Jesus' clothes became dazzling white. The three friends saw Moses and Elijah (great leaders of long ago) talking to Jesus. Then God spoke: 'This is my beloved son. Listen to him.' God was telling them that Jesus had the same kingly power as God himself.

Jesus talks to Moses and Elijah

ZACCHAEUS

AND OTHERS JESUS MET

'Don't bother me now, I'm busy!'

We often say, 'Don't bother me now, I'm busy!' But Jesus never said that to anyone. He had time for everybody, even those that most people didn't like, such as tax-collectors. Tax-collectors were hated because they worked for the Romans, and often overcharged people.

A TAX-COLLECTOR

Zacchaeus could not see Jesus

Zacchaeus was the chief tax-collector in Jericho. He longed to see Jesus when he came to the city, but there was a crowd, and Zacchaeus was not very tall. Zacchaeus knew that the crowd would not let him get near Jesus, so he ran on ahead and climbed into a tree.

Jesus stopped right under the tree. 'Come down, Zacchaeus. I must stay at your house today,' he said, to Zacchaeus' great surprise.

Zacchaeus was overjoyed, and said, 'Lord, here and now I'm giving half my money to the poor, and if I've cheated anybody out of anything, I'll pay it back four times over.' Jesus was very happy. He said, 'I've come to seek and save the lost.'

Bible Search

- A widow: *Luke 7:11–17*
- Bartimaeus: *Luke 18:35–42*
- Zacchaeus: *Luke 19:1–10*

A WIDOW

Jesus was going into the town of Nain, when a funeral procession came out of the town gates.

The dead person was the only son of a widow. Jesus felt extremely sorry for her. He said, 'Don't cry.' He went up to the coffin, which didn't have a lid, and said, 'Young man, get up.' The widow's son was brought back to life.

A JERICHO BEGGAR

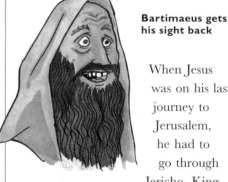

Bartimaeus gets his sight back

When Jesus was on his last journey to Jerusalem, he had to go through Jericho. King Herod had built a fine new town to the south of the old city of Jericho. A blind beggar called Bartimaeus was sitting by the roadside just outside the new town.

Bartimaeus started to call out to Jesus. 'Oh, be quiet!' the crowd said. Jesus stood still. 'What do you want me to do?' Jesus asked. 'Sir, give me my sight back,' Bartimaeus said. 'Your faith has healed you,' Jesus replied.

Jesus brings the young man back to life

JESUS' ENEMIES

Lazarus

Jesus went around doing good. He healed people who were ill, and taught about God. He never tried to stir up rebellion against the Romans who occupied the country. Yet almost all the Jewish leaders wanted to get rid of him. Those who hated the Romans, and those who didn't mind them, all joined forces to kill him. Here are some of the reasons why.

CLAIMING TO BE GOD

Jesus forgives a man's sins

'Your sins are forgiven,' Jesus said to a man lying flat on a stretcher. The Pharisees muttered, 'That's blasphemy. Only God can forgive sins.'

Jewish law said that the punishment for making yourself equal to God was stoning.

- Jesus' claim to be God: *Mark 2:1–12; John 8:58–59*
- Breaking rules: *Mark 3:1–6*
- Crisis: *John 11:45–50*
- Troublemaker: *Mark 11:12–18*

BREAKING RULES

One Sabbath, Jesus healed a man with a crippled arm. The Pharisees were furious, because Jesus had broken the rule about working on the Sabbath. (That was the day they first started plotting to kill Jesus.)

The Pharisees thought that the way to get into heaven was to keep the thousands of rules set out by teachers of the Bible.

Jesus showed that they were wrong, and that what God wanted from people was love and forgiveness.

Jesus heals

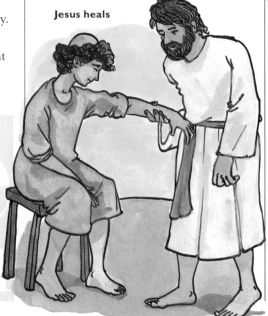

TOO MUCH POWER

In Bethany, just outside Jerusalem, Jesus' friend Lazarus died. Jesus brought him back to life. It was the talk of Jerusalem. This led the Pharisees to join forces with the Sadducees.

The Sadducees were the leading group on the Sanhedrin (a council of religious leaders in Jerusalem). They loved power, and were friendly with the Romans. Usually Pharisees and Sadducees were enemies, but the problem of Jesus was a crisis they needed to work on together to solve.

THE SANHEDRIN

The Sanhedrin held an emergency meeting. They said: 'If we let Jesus go on like this, everyone will believe in him, and the Romans will come and take away both our place and our nation.'

Caiaphas, the High Priest, said, 'It is better that one man die for the people than that the whole nation die.'

JESUS
COMES TO JERUSALEM

After Jesus was baptized, three years went by. By now he was famous. His friends knew he was the Messiah, the great king. They couldn't understand why he said he must die. 'A prophet has to die in Jerusalem,' Jesus said, and set off. Jesus had been to Jerusalem before, but this time was to be different. Christians always remember this day as 'Palm Sunday'.

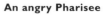

An angry Pharisee

The Pharisees were furious, and tried to make the people keep quiet. But Jesus said, 'If they keep quiet, the stones will cry out.' He was throwing down a challenge to his enemies.

A PROPHECY

When Jesus rode over the top of the Mount of Olives and saw Jerusalem ahead, he wept. 'One day,' he said, 'you will be in ruins.' Forty years later, Jesus' words came true.

Bible Search

- Death in Jerusalem: *Luke 13:33*

- Is he here?: *John 11:55–56*

- Palm Sunday: *Mark 11:1–10*

THE PASSOVER

It was spring, and nearly time for the Passover festival. Every adult Jew was supposed to go to Jerusalem for the Passover. The population of the city grew to six times its normal size. All the nearby villages were crowded, and many visitors slept in tents outside the city walls.

ON THE LOOK-OUT

A donkey for Jesus

In Jerusalem, everyone was looking out for Jesus, and wondering whether he would come. The Pharisees sent out their spies.

.Jesus sent two of his friends ahead of him to Bethany. 'As you enter the town you'll see a young donkey,' he said. 'Untie it and bring it to me.' Jesus planned to ride the last part of the journey into Jerusalem.

THE KING COMES

Five hundred years earlier, an Old Testament preacher had written: 'Shout, daughter of Jerusalem! See your king comes to you… gentle and riding on a donkey.' Everyone knew these words.

The road into Jerusalem was crowded. Many people knew Jesus. When they saw him on the donkey, they tore down branches from the palm trees, and put their cloaks on the road. They yelled, 'Blessed is the king who comes in the name of the Lord.'

Palm Sunday

JESUS' LAST WEEK

Jerusalem was a dangerous place

During the week-long Passover holiday, Jerusalem was a dangerous place to be in. Many Jews were boiling with hatred against the Romans. Armed freedom fighters moved among the crowds. There had recently been one uprising against Rome, and its leaders were still in prison. The city was ready for another rebellion. We can piece together something about every day of Jesus' last week.

SUNDAY

Jesus rode into Jerusalem amid cheering crowds. He looked around the Temple, and then left with his friends to spend the night in Bethany.

MONDAY

The Temple building stood in a vast courtyard. This was the only place where non-Jews could pray. Here money-changers had set up their scales, and traders sold lambs and birds for Temple sacrifices. They often charged too much and made an unfair profit.

Jesus knew what he had to do. He strode into the Temple and threw them all out. 'You've turned the house of prayer into a robbers' den!' he shouted.

This was the very thing the Old Testament preachers had said the Messiah would do. The religious leaders trembled. 'We must kill him,' they said.

Jesus spent the night back in Bethany.

Jesus throws the traders out of the Temple

Bible Search

- A true forecast:
Malachi 3:1–3; Zechariah 14:21

- A robber's den:
Mark 11:15–19

- Traitor:
Mark 14:10–11

TUESDAY

Jesus went back to the Temple courtyard and talked to the crowds of people. The Pharisees and Sadducees tried to trap him with trick questions, but he was too clever for them.

WEDNESDAY

Jesus' enemies were desperate. Jesus was a hero. If they arrested him now, there would be a riot. They couldn't believe their luck when one of Jesus' disciples turned traitor.

The traitor was Judas. He told the enemies: 'I'll take you to him, when there are no crowds.' They agreed to give Judas thirty silver pieces as a reward.

Turn to the next page to find out what happened during the next few days.

JESUS' LAST SUPPER

Jesus' enemies wanted him out of the way before the Passover festival started. Jesus arranged to have the Passover meal with his friends. He made careful plans. 'Go into the city,' he said to two disciples. 'You will see a man with a water pot. He will lead you to an upstairs room. There you can get our meal ready.'

A man directs the disciples to an upstairs room

A SLAVE'S WORK

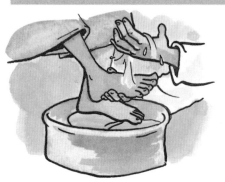

Before the meal started, Jesus washed his friends' feet. This was the work a slave normally did. Jesus said, 'Never forget, you must be servants to one another.'

A WARNING

Jesus knew there was an informer among his friends. He said, 'One of you will betray me.' All the disciples began talking at once. John whispered, 'Who is it?' Jesus said quietly, 'It's the man I give this bread to,' and he gave a piece of bread to Judas. Then Judas went out into the night.

Peter announced, 'I'll die for you.' Jesus said, 'Peter, before the cock crows, you'll have said three times that you don't know me.'

REMEMBER

Then Jesus broke some bread and gave it to his friends. He said, 'This is my body, given for you.' He passed round a cup of wine, and said, 'This is my blood poured out for you, for the forgiveness of sins.' (See also the page on the Lord's Supper.)

Jesus breaks bread and gives it to his friends

LAST ORDERS

John gives up five chapters of his Gospel to Jesus' teaching during that last meal.

'You must love one another,' Jesus said. 'When I am gone, the Holy Spirit, the Helper, will come to be with you.'

The next day, when the Passover lambs were killed, Jesus was killed. By his death and by rising again, he would set his people free from the power of evil.

- A secret sign:
Mark 14:13–15

- Foot-washing:
John 13:1–17

- Judas and Peter:
John 13:18–38

- The Lord's Supper:
Luke 22:14–23

Bible Search

JESUS UNDER ARREST

L ate in the evening after the Passover meal, Jesus and his friends left Jerusalem. In the darkness they crossed the deep Kidron Valley, and climbed the Mount of Olives. At the Garden of Gethsemene, Jesus told his friends to stay awake while he went to pray.

Jesus prays

JESUS PRAYS

Horror and a terrible sadness filled Jesus. He knelt down. 'Everything is possible for you,' he prayed to God, 'Let this pass away. But may your will be done, not mine.' Jesus went back to his friends, but they had fallen asleep. Three times he woke them, but they couldn't stay awake while he prayed.

Bible Search

- Praying: *Mark 14:32–42*
- Arrest: *Mark 14:43–52*
- Annas: *John 18:12–14*
- Sanhedrin: *Mark 14:53–65*
- Peter: *Mark 14:66–72*

ARREST

Judas kisses Jesus

Suddenly, lights and noise filled the garden. Judas arrived, followed by Temple guards armed with swords and clubs. Judas kissed Jesus. This was a sign for the guards to arrest Jesus. Peter struck out with a sword and cut off the ear of one of the guards. But Jesus rebuked Peter and healed the man's ear.

Terrified by what was happening, the disciples ran away.

ON TRIAL

Jesus was taken away and immediately put on trial. This lasted many hours. The Gospel writers summarized what happened during that long night in slightly different ways, but here are some of the main events.

First, Jesus was questioned by Annas, the father-in-law of the High Priest. He was then brought before the Sanhedrin (a council of religious leaders). Witnesses were produced to give evidence against Jesus, but their accounts contradicted each other. During the trial, Jesus watched and said nothing.

Witnesses gave contradictory evidence

ALL NIGHT LONG

The trial by the Sanhedrin lasted a long time. At last the High Priest asked, 'Are you the Messiah, the son of God?' 'I am,' replied Jesus. There was uproar! This was all the evidence that they needed.

Blasphemy such as this was a crime punishable by death.

Outside in the courtyard, Peter denied knowing Jesus.

JESUS PRISONER OF ROME

Roman law did not allow the Jews to put anyone to death. The Jewish leaders had to take Jesus to the Roman governor, Pontius Pilate. They hurried through the streets to King Herod's old palace, which was where Pilate was staying.

Pilate hated Jews.

PILATE

'Jesus is a dangerous man,' the Jews said to Pilate. 'He says he's the king of the Jews. He's stirred up trouble in Galilee.' Jesus wouldn't defend himself.

When Pilate learned Jesus was a Galilean, he sent him to Herod Antipas, ruler of Galilee, who was also staying in the palace.

HEROD ANTIPAS

Herod Antipas questioned Jesus, but Jesus remained silent. So Jesus was sent back to Pilate.

Before Jesus returned to Pilate, the Jewish leaders gathered together a mob that they paid to speak against Jesus.

Jesus remains silent

JESUS SPEAKS TO PILATE

Pilate questions Jesus

'Are you king of the Jews?' asked Pilate. 'The word is yours,' said Jesus. 'My kingdom is not of this world. Everyone on the side of truth listens to me.' Pilate was sure that Jesus was innocent.

Every Passover festival, a prisoner was set free. Pilate decided that this would be Jesus, and he told the crowd he would let Jesus off with a flogging. But the crowd demanded, 'Set Barabbas free!' (Barabbas was another prisoner, a murderer.) 'Crucify Jesus,' they shouted. In the crowd was the mob paid by the Jewish leaders to speak against Jesus.

The crowd demands Jesus' crucifixion

DEATH SENTENCE

Pilate washes his hands of Jesus

Pilate did all he could to set Jesus free. The Jews said, 'If you let him go, you're no friend of Caesar.' This was a threat, meaning that if he did this, Pilate would be shown to be disloyal to the Roman emperor, Caesar.

In the end, Pilate gave in. He took a bowl of water and washed his hands. 'I'm innocent of this man's death,' he stated. He handed Jesus over to be crucified.

Bible Search

- Pilate and Herod:
Luke 23:1–12

- Jesus and Pilate:
John 18:28–19:16

- Pilate washes his hands:
Matthew 27:24

JESUS DIES

D eath by crucifixion was a hideous torture. Cicero, a Roman writer, called it 'the most cruel and revolting punishment'. Yet Jesus had an extra pain to bear as well. As he hung on the cross, he carried the sin which separated people from God.

Jesus carries the cross through the streets of Jerusalem

IN JERUSALEM

Jesus was made to carry the heavy wooden cross on which he would be crucified, through the streets of Jerusalem and out of the city gates. He fell down, and Simon from Cyrene was forced to help carry the cross.

GOLGOTHA

Jesus was taken to Golgotha, which means 'the place of the skull'. Some women offered him a pain-killing drink, but he refused it. The soldiers nailed his hands to the cross. A block of wood half-way up the cross took the weight of his body (or the nails would have torn through his flesh). His feet were tied or nailed to the cross. Over his head, a notice in three languages said: 'The king of the Jews'.

THIEVES

Two thieves were crucified with Jesus. One made fun of him. The other said, 'We deserve our fate, but this man is innocent.' And he said to Jesus, 'Remember me when you come to your kingdom.' Jesus replied, 'Today you will be with me in paradise.'

Bible Search

- In Jerusalem: *Luke 23:26–31*
- Forgive them: *Luke 23:34*
- Mary: *John 19:25–27*
- Jesus' death: *Luke 23:44–49; Matthew 27:45–56*

DARKNESS

Jesus prayed, 'Father forgive them. They don't know what they are doing.' At midday, the sky turned black. For three hours, there was darkness. At three o'clock Jesus cried out, 'My God, my God, why have you left me?' (This was a quotation from Psalm 22.)

Then Jesus shouted, 'It is finished. Into your hands I give my spirit.' And in this way, with a clear mind, and with a prayer, Jesus gave himself to God and died.

When one of the Roman guards saw how Jesus had died, he said, 'Surely this was the son of God.'

Jesus is crucified

JESUS
THE EMPTY TOMB

'If Jesus Christ has not been raised, our preaching is useless, and so is your faith.' These were Paul's words.

We cannot go back into the past and see for ourselves what happened to Jesus, but we can examine the evidence. If Jesus did not rise from the dead, what did happen? Here are some theories.

DISCIPLES

Did the disciples steal the body?
The evidence:
• They were too scared. They all ran away.

• Some were put in prison and killed for preaching that Jesus was alive. Would they have died for a lie?
• If only one or two of them stole the body, how was it that so many saw Jesus alive?

Prison keys

• Roman soldiers guarded the tomb. They would have been punished by death if they had fallen asleep on duty.

Did the guards fall asleep?

THIEVES

Did thieves steal the body?
The evidence:
• What was the point?
• Roman soldiers guarded the tomb.

What's the point?

JESUS

Maybe Jesus was not dead?
The evidence:
• But how did he get out of the tomb? He was exhausted even before he was crucified, and couldn't have moved the stone in front of the tomb. What did he wear? The grave clothes were left behind.
• Would Jesus have preached a lie (that he had risen from the dead)?

• Roman soldiers were sure he was dead.

WOMEN

Perhaps the women went to the wrong tomb?
The evidence:
• In that case, why didn't the Jews produce the body from the right tomb?

A LIE

Perhaps someone made it all up years later?
The evidence:
• The disciples changed from terrified followers to brave preachers. Something made them change.
• The Gospel accounts seem to contradict each other in some details. If they had been invented, the writers would have made sure the stories all agreed.
• The first witnesses were women. No Jew would have made that up. It had to be true!

OTHER EVIDENCE

The Jewish leaders said the body was stolen. If the body was there all the time, why did they put out this story?

CONCLUSION

Conclusion: everyone has to decide for himself or herself.

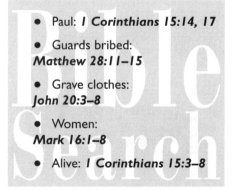

Bible Search

• Paul: *I Corinthians 15:14, 17*
• Guards bribed: *Matthew 28:11–15*
• Grave clothes: *John 20:3–8*
• Women: *Mark 16:1–8*
• Alive: *I Corinthians 15:3–8*

JESUS' SPIRIT IS HERE

Just before he went back to heaven, Jesus said to his friends, 'I am going to send you what my Father has promised. But stay in the city until you have been clothed with power from on high.' What did that mean? The friends had to wait!

DISCIPLES

Jesus' disciples were staying in a large upstairs room, and also spending a lot of time at the Temple. In the Temple there were many small rooms, and they may have rented one of these. Every day, 120 Christians met together to pray and praise God. Jesus' mother was there, and so were his brothers.

Jesus' family

PENTECOST

Ten days went by. Jerusalem was crowded: visitors had come from all over the world for the festival of Passover.

It was early in the morning. The disciples were all together in the room where they were staying. Suddenly, a tremendous wind roared through the house, and fire flashed around them. A flame rested over each disciple, and they were filled with the Holy Spirit.

Visitors came from all over the world for Passover

Bible Search

- An upstairs room: **Acts 1:12, 12:12**

- Wait in Jerusalem: **Luke 24:49; Acts 1:4–5**

- The Holy Spirit: **Acts 2:1–13**

- Peter's sermon: **Acts 2:14–41**

The disciples suddenly found they were able to speak different languages. They went out into the streets, where they were able to speak to people from other countries in their own languages. People were amazed, and asked, 'What's going on? These men are from Galilee, but they're speaking our language!'

A SERMON

Peter stood up and spoke to the crowd. 'This is the Holy Spirit. He's come to us, just as the prophet Joel promised.' And Peter told them all about Jesus, how he had died, and risen again.

That day, 3,000 people became Christians.

WHITSUN

The day the Christian Church began is often called Whitsun, which is short for White Sunday. In the past, new believers were baptized on that day, and always wore white clothes.

A flame appears above each disciple

JESUS IS KING

The resurrection showed that Jesus is God's perfect son: if he had been just an imperfect human, he would have stayed dead. Paul said, 'He was declared with power to be the son of God, by his resurrection from the dead.' When his friends saw Jesus on Easter Sunday evening, they touched him. Jesus ate some fish. This proved he was certainly not a ghost.

Jesus ate some fish

ALIVE!

The Gospels tell us about eleven meetings people had with Jesus when he was brought back to life.

Meeting:	At the empty tomb
Date:	Early Sunday
People:	Women friends
Place in Bible:	Matthew 28:1–10

Meeting:	Outside the tomb
Date:	Early Sunday
People:	Mary Magdelane
Place in Bible:	Mark 16:9–11; John 20:11–18

Mary Magdelene

Meeting:	On the road to Emmaus
Date:	Sunday, midday
People:	Cleopas
Place in Bible:	Luke 24:13–32

Meeting:	In Jerusalem
Date:	Sunday
People:	Peter
Place in Bible:	Luke 24:34; 1 Corinthians 15:5

Meeting:	The upper room, Jerusalem
Date:	Sunday evening
People:	10 disciples, Cleopas
Place in Bible:	Luke 24:36–43; John 20:19–25

Meeting:	The upper room, Jerusalem
Date:	One week later
People:	11 disciples
Place in Bible:	John 20: 26–31

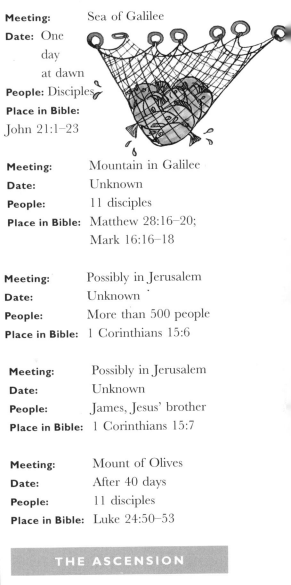

Meeting:	Sea of Galilee
Date:	One day at dawn
People:	Disciples
Place in Bible:	John 21:1–23

Meeting:	Mountain in Galilee
Date:	Unknown
People:	11 disciples
Place in Bible:	Matthew 28:16–20; Mark 16:16–18

Meeting:	Possibly in Jerusalem
Date:	Unknown
People:	More than 500 people
Place in Bible:	1 Corinthians 15:6

Meeting:	Possibly in Jerusalem
Date:	Unknown
People:	James, Jesus' brother
Place in Bible:	1 Corinthians 15:7

Meeting:	Mount of Olives
Date:	After 40 days
People:	11 disciples
Place in Bible:	Luke 24:50–53

THE ASCENSION

Forty days after Easter Sunday, Jesus and the disciples were on the Mount of Olives. As Jesus was praying for them, he was lifted up into the sky, hidden by a cloud. The cloud represented the presence and glory of God. In this way, Jesus showed his friends that he had gone to heaven.

CHRISTIANS THE FIRST

It was exciting to be one of the first Christians, for you never knew what was going to happen next. In the Book of Acts, Luke described some of the events of those early days.

The apostles wanted everyone in Jerusalem to believe in Jesus. Every day, they went to the great outer courtyard of the Temple, where they told everyone who would listen that Jesus was alive.

The apostles tell everyone about Jesus

HOMES

The Christians met in each other's homes. They prayed together and prepared meals, and the special 'Lord's Supper' which Jesus had told them to eat. The Christians shared everything: food, homes and money. Some of the richer people sold houses and land, and the money was given out to Christians with no money.

The people of Jerusalem liked and respected the early Christians, and more and more people became believers.

Bible Search

- Healing a beggar:
  Acts 3:1–10
- Sharing:
  Acts 2:42–47; 4:32–36
- Prison:
  Acts 5:17–42

MIRACLES

Some amazing healing miracles took place. Sick people were brought into the streets on mats, just so that Peter's shadow could fall on them.

Peter heals the sick

Peter healed a lame man outside the Temple, and then preached about Jesus. The Temple police put him in jail. The next day, the Temple leaders held an emergency meeting. 'You must stop this preaching!' they said. But Peter insisted, 'We cannot help speaking about what we have seen and heard.'

The Temple leaders were worried

ESCAPE FROM PRISON

One night two apostles were thrown in prison, but an angel set them free! The next morning, they went straight back to the Temple to see the Temple leaders. 'We must obey God, not you!' Peter said. 'You killed Jesus and God raised him from the dead. We saw it ourselves.'

The leaders were horrified and said, 'We must kill these men.' But a Pharisee called Gamaliel said, 'Leave the men alone. You might find yourselves fighting God.' So Peter and the others were flogged and set free. The flogging was nasty, but the apostles were glad to suffer for Jesus.

Peter is flogged

70

STEPHEN
DIES FOR
HIS BELIEFS

God wanted his message spread all over the world

After Jesus had returned to heaven, the apostles at first stayed in Jerusalem. They preached to the people, and went to the Temple. But God had bigger plans for them than that, which he set in motion through three men: Stephen, Peter (see the page on Cornelius) and Paul.

- God didn't need the Temple.
- They were the ones who had not kept God's laws.
- They had betrayed and murdered God's chosen leader.

STEPHEN

The twelve apostles were very busy, so seven men were chosen to be in charge of money and food. One of these men was Stephen. He was one of the first people to see that the Christian faith was for the whole world.

Stephen performed many miracles among the people. He also preached that trust in Jesus meant that the Temple, and many Jewish laws, were no longer needed. This was dangerous teaching! Stephen was arrested, and brought before the Sanhedrin (the council of religious leaders), just as Jesus had been.

Stephen was in charge of money and food

Jesus carries his cross

DEATH

The council members were absolutely furious. Stephen said, 'Look, I see heaven open and Jesus standing at the right hand of God.' At this, they dragged Stephen out of the city and stoned him to death. As he lay dying, he cried, 'Lord, do not hold this sin against them.'

PERSECUTION

After this, many Christians were thrown into prison, and many left Jerusalem and went to live in other towns. Everywhere they went, they talked about Jesus. The more people tried to destroy the new faith, the more it spread!

Bible Search
- Choosing the seven: *Acts 6:1–7*
- Stephen: *Acts 6:8–15*
- Stephen's speech: *Acts 7:1–53*
- Death: *Acts 7:54–60*

STEPHEN'S DEFENCE

Luke wrote that Stephen's face looked like the face of an angel. His speech to the Sanhedrin was so important that Luke quoted a long section of it in Acts. At first, the speech reads like a history lesson telling the story of the Jews. At the end of the speech, Stephen delivers three bombshells to the Sanhedrin. He told them:

PETER THE DISCIPLE

Peter, the 'rock'

P eter was one of Jesus' twelve disciples. His real name was Simon. Jesus gave him the nickname 'Peter', which meant 'rock'. At first Peter wasn't very strong in his beliefs. He was more like shifting sand than rock! But Jesus said to him, 'I have prayed for you.' We see how Peter grew strong and became, as Paul later wrote, a 'pillar' of the Church.

Shifting sand

EARLY DAYS

Peter and his brother Andrew were supporters of John the Baptist. Jesus came to John to be baptized. Andrew met Jesus and knew that he wanted to follow him, so he rushed to tell his brother.

Later, by the Sea of Galilee, Jesus found Peter and Andrew at work fishing. 'Follow me and I will make you fishers of men,' Jesus said. They went with Jesus straight away.

A COWARD

Before he was arrested, Jesus told his disciples that one of them would betray him. When Peter said this was impossible, Jesus turned to him and said, 'Before the cock crows at dawn, you will have disowned me three times.' That night, Jesus was arrested. Peter, along with John, followed Jesus right into the courtyard of the High Priest's house.

Three different people came up and asked Peter if he was one of Jesus' followers. Each time, Peter denied that he was.

Jesus beckons Peter and Andrew to follow him

A LEADER

When Jesus was brought back to life after being crucified, he met Peter and forgave him.

When Jesus returned to heaven, the disciples continued to spread God's word. They became known as the apostles. Peter was beaten, and thrown into prison because he kept on preaching about Jesus. He was one of the first to see that the Christian faith was for everyone, not just for Jews. But he didn't always have the courage to practice what he preached. (See the pages on the First Christians and on Cornelius.)

Peter wrote two letters, which can be found in the Bible as 1 and 2 Peter, to help Christians. His life ended when he was crucified in Rome.

- Who am I?:
Matthew 16:16

- Jesus' prayer:
Luke 22:32

- Christianity for all:
Acts 10:9–48

Bible Search

CORNELIUS
SHOWS CHRIST IS FOR ALL PEOPLE

Cornelius

Cornelius was a Roman officer living in Caesarea, where he was in charge of a hundred soldiers. He was a good man, who prayed regularly and helped anybody in need. One day, an angel came to Cornelius and said, 'God has heard your prayers and seen your good deeds. Now, send some men to Joppa to find Peter.'

DOUBLE VISION

Peter was praying when he saw a large sheet, tied at the four corners, coming down from the sky. Inside were all sorts of animals, reptiles and birds.

A voice said, 'Kill them and eat.' 'But I can't,' protested Peter. 'Some are unclean.' (Foods forbidden to the Jews were known as 'unclean'.) The voice replied, 'Do not call something unclean when God calls it clean.'

Peter saw the vision twice more, before Cornelius' men arrived.

Peter's vision

VISITORS

The Holy Spirit said to Peter, 'These men are looking for you. I've sent them.' Then Peter understood the vision. Until then, like all Jews, Peter had thought that non-Jews were 'unclean'. A Jew wouldn't even go into the house of a non-Jew. Now God was changing all that. Peter welcomed the men into his house.

THE HOLY SPIRIT

The next day, Peter went to Cornelius' house. He began to preach to Cornelius, his family and friends, about Jesus. Then the Holy Spirit filled the house, and all the Romans began to praise Jesus. The Jews with Peter were amazed, because the Holy Spirit had come to people who weren't Jewish. Peter baptized Cornelius and all his family.

The Romans praise Jesus

A TURNING POINT

That was a turning point in the life of the Church. Later on, Christians held a meeting in Jerusalem to talk about whether Gentiles (non-Jews) could be Christians. Peter said, 'God has shown me that all people, Jews and Gentiles, may be saved. All they need to do is believe in Jesus.'

(See also the pages on Stephen and Paul.)

Bible Search

- The angel: *Acts 10:1–7*
- Peter's vision: *Acts 10:9–23*
- Peter visits Cornelius: *Acts 10:23–48*
- The council of Jerusalem: *Acts 15:1–35*

PAUL MEETS JESUS

More than one third of the New Testament was written by Paul. Yet at first, Paul detested all Christians. The story of how Paul changed, became a Christian, and spread the teachings of Christianity is told three times in the Book of Acts. This shows what a revolutionary story it was.

Saul as a student

GROWING UP

Paul is a Roman name. Paul grew up as a Jew in Tarsus, an important Greek city. Paul's Jewish name was Saul. Saul learned the trade of leather-worker and tentmaker. He also went on to higher education in Jerusalem, where he became a student of the famous teacher Gamaliel. Saul was brilliant, and had a great future as one of the country's leading Pharisees.

Saul learned to make tents and work with leather

- Education: *Acts 22:2–3*
- Paul sees Stephen stoned: *Acts 7:57–8:1*
- Paul sees Jesus, told by Luke: *Acts 9:3–19*
- Told by Paul: *Acts 22:6–16; 26:9–23*

CHRISTIANS

In Saul's view, Christians were ignorant, dangerous people who told lies about God. Saul made up his mind to stamp out the Christian faith. He set off for the city of Damascus, with warrants for the arrest of all the Christians.

Just outside Damascus, a very bright light suddenly shone from the sky. A voice called, 'Saul, why do you persecute me?' Saul fell to the ground. 'Who are you?' he asked. 'I am Jesus,' said the voice. 'Go into the city and you will be told what to do.'

Saul falls to the ground

BLINDED

Saul stood up, and found he couldn't see. The men with him led him into Damascus. For the next three days, Saul didn't eat or drink. He was shattered, realizing that the Jesus he had despised, and who had been crucified, was alive.

ANANIAS

Ananias heals Saul

Jesus sent a man called Ananias to Saul. Ananias said, 'In the name of Jesus, receive your sight.' Saul was baptized. From that moment on, he began to preach about Jesus.

He travelled throughout the Roman empire.

After Saul converted to Christianity, he became known by his Roman name of Paul.

PAUL TIME CHART

P aul was a man under orders. When he met Jesus on the road to Damascus, his life was turned around. His new aim in life was to complete the task Jesus had given him. That task was to preach the good news of Jesus to Jews and non-Jews throughout the Roman world.

Paul meets Jesus.

Paul is baptized in Damascus.

Brief visit to 'Arabia'. **(Galatians 1:17)**

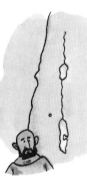

AD 35. Paul preaches in Damascus for three years. **(2 Corinthians 11:32; Galatians 1:17)**

Visit to Jerusalem. The Christians think his new faith is a trick! Barnabas makes friends with Paul. **(Galatians 1:18; Acts 9:23–28)**

Return to Tarsus. Paul spends eleven years preaching in the area.

AD 42. Barnabas asks Paul to help him in Antioch. **(Acts 11:19–26)**

AD 43. Paul and Barnabas go to Jerusalem with gifts of money. At a private meeting, the Jerusalem Christians support Paul's work among non-Jews. **(Acts 11:27–30; Galatians 2:1–10)**

Back at Antioch, the Christians send Paul and Barnabas on a missionary tour. **(Acts 13–14)**

AD 46–48. Return to Antioch. Paul hears that Christians from Jerusalem have gone to the new churches, saying all Christians must become Jews. Paul is horrified. He writes to the Christians in Galatia.

AD 49. To Jerusalem for a conference to discuss the problems. (See the page on Cornelius.)

AD 50–52. Paul and Silas set off from Antioch on a second missionary tour. He writes 1 and 2 Thessalonians.

Return to Antioch. **(Acts 18:22)**

AD 53–57. Third missionary trip. Paul spends three years in Ephesus. He writes 1 and 2 Corinthians and Romans.

AD 57–59. Paul and his friends go to Jerusalem with more money. Paul is arrested and spends two years as a prisoner. He appeals to Caesar. **(Acts 23–26)**

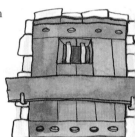

AD 59. Paul is shipwrecked on the way to Rome, and spends the winter on Malta. **(Acts 27–28:10)**

AD 60–62. House arrest, probably in Rome. Paul writes letters to Philemon and to Christians in Colosse, Philippi and Ephesus. The Book of Acts ends here.

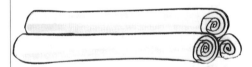

AD 62. This is the likely date Paul was set free. He visits his friends in the churches. He writes letters to Timothy and Titus. He may have gone on to Spain.

AD 64 or later. Paul is back in Rome, where he is imprisoned again. He is killed on the orders of Emperor Nero.

PAUL ON TOUR

The Christian faith started off from a small group of Jews in Jerusalem. Thirty years later, it had spread throughout the Roman world. This drastic change was managed by Paul. We know about Paul's adventures and travels from the diary Luke kept (given in the Book of Acts).

PAUL'S METHOD

• Paul didn't try to do it alone. He always took at least one helper with him.
• He headed for the important cities, which were centres of communication.
• In each town, he went to the Jews first, then to the non-Jews.
• He revisited the new Christians, and sent letters and teachers to help them understand their new faith.
• He didn't ask for money. When he was short of funds, he worked as a tentmaker.

Paul healed a cripple, and was worshipped as a god.

Mark gave up.

Here the Roman governor became a Christian.

Travelling was hard and dangerous. Paul walked, or rode a donkey. He wrote that he had been in danger from bandits, and from rivers. He was shipwrecked three times.

Bible Search

• Tour 1: *Acts 13:4–14:28*
• Tour 2: *Acts 15:36–18:22*
• Tour 3: *Acts 18:23–21:17*
• Tough times: *2 Corinthians 11:23–29*

TOUR ONE

Lystra

Perga

Cyprus

TOUR TWO

Phillipi

Troas

Paul sang hymns in jail. The jailer believed in Jesus.

In a vision, Paul saw a man begging him to go to Macedonia.

TOUR THREE

There was a riot, started by silversmiths who sold images of the goddess Diana.

Ephesus

PAUL SPEAKS

T he previous pages on Paul may have given you some ideas about what he was like. We know how brave he was; how hard he worked for Jesus; how full of love he was for Jesus and for other people (though he had a quick temper!) Here are a few more glimpses, from some of the things he said about himself.

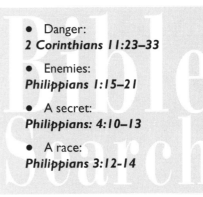

Bible Search

- Danger:
  2 Corinthians 11:23–33
- Enemies:
  Philippians 1:15–21
- A secret:
  Philippians: 4:10–13
- A race:
  Philippians 3:12–14

PAUL'S WORK

'I always want to preach the good news in places where people have never heard of Jesus.'

DANGEROUS JOURNEYS

'Five times, the Jews have given me their punishment of thirty-nine lashes with a whip. Three different times I was beaten with rods…many times I have been without food. I have been cold and without clothes…'

Paul was beaten…

…starved

…cold and without clothes

ENEMIES

'I do not care if they make trouble for me… To me the only important thing about living is Christ.'

A SECRET

The secret of being happy

'I have learned the secret of being happy at any time in everything that happens…when I have all that I need, and when I do not have the things I need. I can do all things through Christ because he gives me strength.'

'The first time I defended myself no one helped me. Everyone left me…But the Lord stayed with me. He gave me strength…'

LETTERS

Paul may have had bad eyesight. His friends often wrote his letters for him. At the end of one letter he wrote: 'I am writing this myself. See what large letters I use.'

A RACE

'I intend to be the kind of man Jesus wanted me to be when he called me on the road to Damascus. I know I haven't got there yet; but I've set my heart on one thing: to forget the past and live for the future. I'm like a long-distance runner; I see the tape ahead and I'm going to get there – and win the prize.'

Paul compared himself to a long-distance runner

PAUL'S FRIENDS

Paul was not a loner. He had a team of close friends who helped in his work. He also had many other Christian friends. When he rounded off his letter to the Christians in Rome, he sent greetings to twenty-eight people by name. Here are some of Paul's team.

Luke

LUKE

Paul described Luke as 'our dear doctor'. He joined Paul on the second journey, and looked after him when he was ill. He wrote the Gospel of Luke and the Book of Acts. He was an excellent writer and an accurate historian.

Barnabas

MARK

Mark set off on Paul's first missionary journey, but gave up after a while and went home.

Barnabas wanted Mark (his cousin) to go with them on their next journey, but Paul refused. So Barnabas went off with Mark, and Paul went with Silas. Later, Mark became Paul's assistant, and also helped Peter. He wrote the Gospel of Mark.

PRISCILLA AND AQUILA

Priscilla and Aquila were a married couple. Paul stayed at their home in Corinth several times, and helped them to make tents. Their house was a meeting place for Christians.

TITUS

Titus was a brave member of the team on Paul's third journey. Paul sent Titus to sort out the trouble in the Church in Corinth. He was successful, so Paul sent him to Crete.

Titus

BARNABAS

When Paul became a Christian and went to Jerusalem, Barnabas helped him to make friends with the other Christians.

Barnabas asked Paul to help him in Antioch. Barnabas and Paul travelled together as missionaries, taking Mark with them.

TIMOTHY

Timothy was one of Paul's closest friends. Paul wrote: 'I have no one else like him...' He first joined Paul on the second journey. Paul wrote the First and Second Letter of Timothy to him.

SILAS

Silas

Silas was one of the leaders in Jerusalem, and went with Paul on his second journey. Paul called him 'a faithful Christian brother'. He also helped Peter.

Bible Search

- Barnabas: *Acts 4:36–37; 9:26–27; 11:25–26*

- Mark: *Acts 15:36–40; Colossians 4:10*

- Timothy: *Acts 16:1–3; 1 and 2 Timothy*

- Luke: *Colossians 4:14; 2 Timothy 4:11*

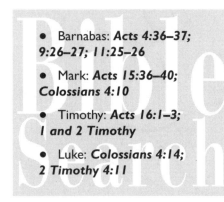
Timothy and Paul

JOHN THE DISCIPLE

John

Jesus nicknamed John and his brother James the 'sons of thunder'. It was probably because they both had a bad temper! When a village wouldn't welcome Jesus, the brothers would say, 'Call down fire from heaven and destroy it!' In the New Testament, we see a change taking place in John, and he becomes less angry.

FISHERMEN

John and his brother James lived in Capernaum, by the Sea of Galilee. They were fishermen. One day, they were mending their nets with their father Zebedee, when they saw Jesus walking towards them. 'Come with me,' Jesus said. At once, they decided to follow him.

Together with Peter, John and James became Jesus' closest friends.

POWER-SEEKING

One day, James and John, encouraged by their mother, asked Jesus: 'May we have the seats of power on your right and left-hand side when you come as king?' The other disciples were furious when they found out!

But John let go of his longing for power. In his Gospel, he didn't even put his name, but just described himself as 'the disciple Jesus loved'.

James and John are encouraged to seek power

JESUS' MOTHER

When Jesus was dying, John stood close to the foot of the cross, next to Mary. Jesus said to John, 'Here is your mother.' And he said to Mary, 'Here is your son.' From then on, John looked after Mary.

COURAGE

When Jesus was raised from the dead, John and Peter went to tell the people of Jerusalem. For this, they were thrown in prison. John and Peter refused to be silenced. 'We cannot help speaking about what we have seen and heard,' they said. It was a dangerous time for the disciples: King Herod arrested James, and had him killed.

John is arrested

THE WRITER

John wrote the Gospel of John and the Book of Revelation. He also wrote three letters, known as 1, 2, and 3 John, when he was an old man living in Ephesus. Above all else, these letters stressed the importance of love.

Bible Search

- Follow Jesus: *Mark 1:19–20*
- Sons of thunder: *Luke 9:51–55*
- Power-seeking: *Mark 10:35–45*
- Love: *1 John 4:7–21*

INDEX